KINGDOM

KINGDOM COME

The Kingdom of God in the Teaching of Jesus

Chris Marshall

Head of the Department of New Testament Studies
Bible College of New Zealand

WIPF & STOCK · Eugene, Oregon

Wipf and Stock Publishers
199 W 8th Ave, Suite 3
Eugene, OR 97401

Kingdom Come
The Kingdom of God in the Teaching of Jesus
By Marshall, Christopher D.
Copyright©1990 by Marshall, Christopher D.
ISBN 13: 978-1-4982-2298-3
Publication date 8/15/2015
Previously published by Impetus, 1990

Contents

Preface

This book is a revised version of a paper delivered to the Theological Commission of the Evangelical Fellowship of New Zealand, January 20, 1987. I have resisted the temptation of substantially rewriting the original paper. The revision has consisted mainly of extending the final section on the social dimensions of the kingdom proclamation of Jesus, and making one or two additions to earlier sections. I have also increased the amount of secondary literature referred to in the notes to enable readers to follow up specific points of interest if they so wish. I have made no attempt to be exhaustive however; I have mainly cited works that should be readily accessible, and understandable, to most readers.

An earlier version of the paper has already appeared in print in the *Christian Brethren Research Fellowship Journal* 120 (1990), 7-25, and as an independent booklet, but I have agreed to publish it in its revised format to make it more widely available. In addition to the major paper on the kingdom of God, I have also included the text of a short meditation, entitled 'The Precious and Costly Kingdom', which I delivered to a *Christian Workers Training Day*, 29 August, 1989. A slightly abbreviated version of this address was first published in the *Reaper* 71, 6 (1989/90), 5-16.

This essay on the kingdom of God is not aimed at New Testament specialists. It is addressed rather to church leaders and informed lay people interested in exploring the biblical roots of the so-called, and rather diverse, 'kingdom theology' movement that is currently influencing many churches in New Zealand and abroad. I have also tried to keep in mind the needs of my first year New Testament students, who soon discover that it is impossible to make much sense out of the ministry of Jesus without understanding his message of the kingdom of God.

Biblical quotations are from the *New Revised Standard Version*

Chris Marshall

Foreword

In the past fifteen years many Christians have rediscovered the kingdom of God. I myself recall the excitement with which I, concordance at the ready, first followed kingdom words throughout the New Testament. What a big vision Jesus was presenting! What surprising and potent works accompanied his teaching! How could I understand and integrate it all? Not surprisingly, I, like most Bible readers, got a partial picture. This picture was enough to energize my mind and will in new truths leading to unfamiliar forms of Christian discipleship. I found this exciting, but also perplexing. Like others, whose kingdom learnings had taken them in other directions, I had made valuable discoveries, but gaps remained.

Today, to my immense gratitude, we can turn to Chris Marshall's *Kingdom Come* to guide us through Jesus' kingdom teaching. The author is a reliable guide. He is a scholar of learning and integrity. I respect his discerning use of the work of other Biblical scholars; indeed, *Kingdom Come* is a valuable introduction to recent scholarship on the kingdom. Furthermore, Dr Marshall is a gifted teacher, who communicates to a wide audience. Ordinary Bible readers as well as theologians can profit from his insights. Most important of all, the author is committed to let the Biblical texts speak clearly, however disconcerting that clarity may be. In the face of Jesus' words and actions that cut to the heart of things, Dr Marshall is determined to be defenceless.

This is the main reason why Chris Marshall has so much to contribute to Christians in the 1990s. Whereas many Christians, in the kingdom of God, have found new ways of justifying their own fragments of the truth, the author has demonstrated that, for Jesus, the kingdom of God was a unifying vision of tantalizing, intriguing wholeness. It was a vision of integrated living under God's sovereignty.

The kingdom of God, Chris Marshall has demonstrated, holds together concerns that we Christians, in our faithlessness, habitually break asunder. In his analysis, three dimensions of God's kingdom are evident in Jesus' teaching and action. God's kingdom comes in his acts of eschatological power, a truth which charismatic Christians celebrate. God's kingdom also brings a sense of the nearness of God, a truth to which Evangelical and contemplative Christians bear testimony. And God's kingdom brings a call to social transformation, a truth which animates the thinking and action of Christian radicals. Jesus, the proclaimer of the kingdom, united these three aspects in his person. What might happen today, Dr Marshall asks, if Christians today discovered this integrative vision and put it to work in their lives as individuals and churches?

We would have to change; as Dr Marshall points out, Jesus' kingdom proclamation always invited people to repent. This repentance might lead to new and surprising reconciliations between previously estranged camps of Christians. It might also lead to new expressions of Christian common life. Dr Marshall sees churches as 'a visible demonstration that God has made a whole new way of life possible.' Imagine congregations who are so sure of God's power and nearness that they can explore new, Jesus-like approaches to the crunch issues of his time and ours — wealth, power, violence, and an impatience with marginal people.

In an era in which only ten per cent of the English people attend church regularly, groups of people experiencing together a kingdom lifestyle of empowered integration might well be God's means of reaching the ninety per cent with surprisingly good news.

Dr Marshall concludes his study with a meditation on Jesus' kingdom parables of the hidden treasure and of the infinitely valuable pearl. These parables, in brief compass, say it all. God's kingdom calls us to disinvest, to discard all allurements and securities that prevent us from responding to God's purposes.

God's kingdom also calls us to invest, to commit the resources of our wealth and desire to the true riches that, under God, bring surprising dividends. Joy, hope, the knowledge that in God all things are possible — these are kingdom treasures that Chris Marshall invites us to discover in this important and inspiring book.

Dr Alan Kreider
Scholar in Residence
Northern Baptist College
and lecturer at Manchester University

1

Introduction

Writing in 1976, the British New Testament scholar I.H. Marshall lamented the fact that in the previous sixteen years he could recall only two sermons specifically on the topic of the kingdom of God, and both of those by recent graduates of theological college.[1] It is hard to imagine him being able to make a similar observation today, only a decade and a half later. For in recent years the theme of the kingdom of God has come to the forefront in the preaching, teaching and popular writing of Christians of all theological persuasions. Indeed in a more recent article on the subject, Marshall speaks no longer of how rare it is to hear the kingdom of God referred to but of how the term is now 'bandied about with great frequency in discussions of Christian social action', although in 'a very vague manner' and without 'clear biblical exposition in the churches on the meaning of the term'.[2] The lack of clarity behind the current attraction for kingdom-language is also underlined by R.T. France.

> If you ask the ordinary 'non-theological' Christian what he understands by 'the kingdom of God' you will probably get no answer at all! If you do get an answer, it is likely to be in terms of 'heaven' or 'life after death'; or it may be something to do with the church. If he is more aware of current debate, he may define it as something to do with social justice, the creation of a new social order. If he has been influenced by liberation theology he may go further and see it as a political slogan for the overthrow of oppressive regimes. If he has a smattering of (old-fashioned) theological knowledge, he may think with Harnack of the brave new world where all men will be brothers and the Sermon on the Mount

---

1   I.H. Marshall, 'Preaching the kingdom of God', *Expository Times* 89 (1977), 13.
2   I.H. Marshall, 'The Hope of a New Age: The kingdom of God in the New Testament', *Themelios* 11,1 (1985), 5

their ethical standard, or with Schweitzer of the cataclysmic inbreaking of God's new order which formed the apocalyptic hope of Jesus and his first followers. All this and more is waiting to be triggered off by the phrase 'the kingdom of God', depending on who hears it; and yet people go on using it as if it had a clear, universally agreed meaning, as if there were 'something' to which it obviously refers, so that there is no need to discuss what sort of phrase it is.[1]

Now any attempt to gain some clarity on the biblical meaning of the phrase 'the kingdom of God' must take the teaching of Jesus as its major point of reference; for the prominence of kingdom-terminology today is directly attributable to the great frequency with which he appealed in his teaching to the notion of God's kingdom. The expression is ubiquitous in the synoptic Gospels. It is found some fifteen times in Mark, fifty-two times in Matthew, and thirty-seven times in Luke, though it is comparatively rare elsewhere in canonical and non-canonical sources. It features in around sixty different sayings of Jesus in the synoptic tradition, and is used by each of the synoptic writers to summarise the essence of Jesus' message.[2] It is therefore universally agreed by New Testament scholars that the kingdom of God was the dominant note in the preaching of the historical Jesus.

This is not to say that the phrase itself is somehow sacred or indispensable. Given Jesus' unique preference for the expression, it is striking how little the later New Testament writers employ it. The term

---

1   R.T. France, 'The Church and the kingdom of God: Some Hermeneutical Issues', in D.A. Carson (ed.), *Biblical Interpretation and the Church: Text and Context* (Exeter: Paternoster, 1984), 31.
2   See Mark 1:14-15; Matt 4:23; 9:35; Luke 4:43; 8:1; 9:11

'kingdom' occurs only fourteen times in the Pauline corpus,[1] and is found only three times in the Fourth Gospel[2] and seven or eight times in Acts.[3] This partly reflects the shift in emphasis that took place between the pre-Easter ministry of Jesus and the post-Easter preaching of the early Church. Whereas Jesus proclaimed the kingdom of God, the first Christians proclaimed the Proclaimer. The royal person[4] in whom the kingdom of God was revealed, rather than the kingdom *per se*, became the dominant focus of the Christian gospel, and metaphors such as 'eternal life', 'salvation' and 'the righteousness of God' were used to express the accomplishment of his life, death and resurrection.

It is not entirely clear why the first Christians made less frequent mention of the kingdom of God in their preaching than Jesus had done in his. One common explanation is that whereas the term was immediately comprehensible in the Palestinian Jewish setting of Jesus' ministry, its meaning would not have been so readily transparent in the wider Hellenistic setting of the early Church. But this cannot be the whole explanation. The notion of divine kingship was not uniquely Jewish; it was widespread in antiquity, although without the distinctively Jewish eschatological qualification. Moreover, the Hellenistic context of the early Christian communities, and their predominantly Gentile make-up, did not prevent Paul and the other New Testament writers from employing a

1   Rom 14:17; 1 Cor 4:20; 6:9-10; 15:24; Gal 5:21; 1 Thess 2:12; 2 Thess 1:5; Eph
        5:5; Col 1:13; 4:11; 2 Tim 4:1, 18
2   John 3:3, 5; cf. 18:36
3   Acts 1:3; 8:12; 14:22; 19:8; 20:25; 28:23, 31; cf. 1:6
4   Cf. Acts 17:7

wide-range of distinctively Jewish metaphors in their explanation of the gospel. On the other hand, even in the New Testament accounts of early Christian preaching to Jewish audiences, where the biblical notion of God's kingdom was directly intelligible, explicit reference to the kingdom is still not frequent. Perhaps it was simply the pressing need to clarify in precisely *what way* the kingdom of God had been realised — covertly in the person and work of the Crucified One — that necessitated the more conspicuous employment of christological (Christ-centred) over theological (kingdom-centred) categories. Yet kingdom language was never abandoned. Even in the epistle to the Romans, where Paul's use of the phrase 'the righteousness of God' is more or less equivalent to Jesus' use of 'the kingdom of God', Paul presumes that the latter concept is well-known and understood by his predominantly Gentile readers (Rom 14:17).[1]

It should be said, then, that there is a genuine continuity between the message of Jesus and the message of the early Church.[2] There are not *two* gospels in the New Testament: the gospel of the kingdom (Mark 1:14f) and the gospel of personal salvation (Rom 1:16f). The gospel of salvation in Christ presupposes, re-expresses and further unpacks the kingdom-preaching and kingdom-establishing ministry of Jesus. While the phrase 'kingdom of God' is not indispensable to New Testament

---

1   As Dunn observes, 'Paul recalls the Roman audience to a phrase which he must
     have assumed was familiar to them also from the common stock of Jesus'
     teaching, which all Christian churches doubtless possessed in one form or
     another', J.D.G. Dunn, *Romans 9-16*, Word Biblical Commentary 38b (Dallas:
     Word, 1988), 822.
2   Cf. B.E. Gärtner, 'The Person of Jesus and the kingdom of God', *Theology Today*
     27, 1970, 32-43.

theology, the underlying notion of the definitive manifestation of God's saving sovereignty in the life and work of Jesus most certainly is.

The aim of the following discussion is not to arrive at a single precise definition of what Jesus meant by 'the kingdom of God'. Jesus used the phrase in so many different linguistic connections[1] and in relation to such a variety of subject matter, that it is virtually impossible to formulate a simple definition of the concept that would encompass all its aspects. The phrase functions in Jesus' teaching as a kind of umbrella term embracing all the diverse ways in which God's eschatological sovereignty impinges on human life. I want instead to point to some of the characteristic features that appear in the kingdom proclamation of Jesus, and then to outline three main emphases in Jesus' teaching which find their point of integration in, and give positive content to, his conception of God's kingdom. It is this integrative or holistic character of the term 'kingdom of God' that is crucial to grasp, both for understanding its meaning in the teaching of Jesus and for determining its relevance for the mission of the Church today.

---

1   J. Jeremias lists eighteen verbal connections employing the phrase 'kingdom of God' in the sayings of Jesus to which there are no known contemporary parallels; and that is not counting those sayings where Jesus speaks of the kingdom in a similar manner to his contemporaries, *New Testament Theology* (London: SCM, 1971), I. 32-34

Method of Approach

I should stress that the ensuing analysis of Jesus' teaching on the kingdom of God is not adressed to New Testament specialists, and does not concern itself with the technicalities of academic Jesus-Research. It seeks rather to integrate and make accessible to ordinary readers the fruits of recent Gospel scholarship.

No attempt has been made to assess the authenticity of the various sayings ascribed to Jesus, nor to delineate the redactional interests of the individual Evangelists.[1] These two concerns have dominated modern Gospel scholarship and there is no denying their importance. As one trained in Gospel criticism, I am keenly aware of the methodological criticisms the approach I employ is open to. But it is my conviction that the redactional activity of the Gospel writers — and the primitive Church that handled the traditions before them — has been largely a matter of giving selective emphasis and interpretive clarity to intrinsic features of Jesus' original teaching.

It is therefore possible, I believe, to derive a fair understanding of Jesus' own perspective on the kingdom of God by surveying the broad range of Gospel data, without attempting to locate the contribution each text makes to the distinctive theology of the individual Evangelists (and vice versa), or seeking to demonstrate the authenticity of each. Certainly the available kingdom-sayings in the Gospels owe their final form and

---

1   For a discussion of the perspectives of each of the Gospel writers on the kingdom of God, see the four essays in chaps 9-12 of Wendell Willis (ed.), *The Kingdom of God in 20th Century Interpretation* (Peabody, MA: Hendrickson Publishers, 1987), 119-174

context to the work of the Gospel writers, and reflect in part the perspective and concerns of these writers. But the leading concern of the Evangelists has been to expound and elucidate for their own readers the unique message of Jesus himself, and ultimately it is *Jesus'* message about God's kingdom that explains and shines through the Gospel material.

In so-called 'Jesus Research', several scholars now eschew the piece-meal approach that strives to peel away redactional modifications from every item of the Gospel tradition and admit only the allegedly 'authentic' residue into the reconstruction of the historical Jesus. Instead, without abandoning entirely tests of authenticity, they rely more upon the total impression gained, cumulatively, from putting side by side all the various traditions of Jesus' words and deeds, in order to arrive at a more or less impressionistic portrait of the one historical personality to whom these diverse traditions attest.[1] In the pluralistic age we live in, many scholars have become so enamoured of the theological diversity of the New Testament writings that they sometimes lose sight of the common themes, emphases and motifs that permeate and unite the different strands of New Testament tradition. For all their individual distinctiveness, all the Gospel traditions focus on the challenge represented in the life and teaching of one single individual, Jesus of Nazareth. And the general theological and ethical outlook of this individual is surely not as difficult to discern behind the Gospel accounts as critical scholarship often suggests.

---

1   See the comments by C.F.D. Moule, *The Origin of Christology* (Cambridge: CUP, 1977), 156-57

New Testament experts and those acquainted with the technicalities of research on the historical Jesus may well find the following survey-method unsatisfying. But at the end of the day, the critical issues that are important for the scholar to pursue are of less interest to the broader Christian readership I have in mind.

2

The Background Setting of Jesus' Proclamation

*T*hat Jesus could make such heavy use of the phrase 'the kingdom of God' without ever defining exactly what he meant by it, indicates that he expected his hearers to understand readily what he was talking about. Although the formula itself was hardly commonplace in the religious language of first-century Palestinian Judaism, the idea of God as king was universally acknowledged and cherished. On the other hand, the fact that Jesus devoted so much of his teaching to explaining the character and implications of God's kingdom suggests that he used the traditional concept chiefly as a point of departure. His own conception differed in crucial ways from prevailing expectations. The search for new images and metaphors to convey this difference underlies much of his parabolic discourse, as Mark 4:30 makes clear: 'with what can we compare the kingdom of God, or what parable will we use for it?' To understand Jesus' message of the kingdom, therefore, we need to examine Old Testament-Jewish expectations and then to trace the distinctive features in Jesus' relation to them.

Old Testament Hope

The expression 'kingdom of God' is not found as such in the Old Testament.[1] However Yahweh is referred to as 'king' on at least forty-one occasions and there are fifteen references to the 'kingdom' which Yahweh

---

1   The precise role of the concept of the kingdom of God in Old Testament theology
     is disputed by Old Testament scholars. See recenly D. Patrick, 'The Kingdom of
     God in the Old Testament', in Wendell Willis (ed.), *The Kingdom of God in
     20th-Century Interpretation* (Peabody, MA: Hendrickson Publishers, 1987),
     67-79; M.J. Selman, 'The Kingdom of God in the Old Testament', *Tyndale
     Bulletin* 40.2 (1989), 161-83.

rules.[1] The emphasis throughout, scholars agree, is on the *ruling activity* of God rather than on the *realm* where God exercises this rule. Talk of God's kingship evokes ideas of sovereignty, power, authority, supremacy, might.

In this Old Testament theology of divine kingship, it is perhaps helpful to distinguish two main lines of thought — Yahweh as the reigning king and Yahweh as the coming king.

(a)   Yahweh the Reigning King

The Old Testament frequently speaks of God as a king who is currently exercising royal rule. The notion of Yahweh as a reigning king is connected both with God's relationship to creation and with God's relationship to Israel. God's dominion over creation is sometimes spoken of in terms of kingship or rule.

> The Lord is king, he is robed in majesty:
> The Lord is robed, he is girded with strength.
> He has established the world;
> it shall never be moved;
> your throne is established from of old;
> you are from everlasting.[2]
>
> Clap your hands, all you peoples;
> shout to God with a loud songs of joy.
> For the Lord, the Most High, is awesome,
> A great king over all the earth.[3]

---

1   See Pss 22:28; 103:19; 145:11-13; 1 Chr 17:14; 28:5; 29:11; 2 Chr 13:8; Obad 21; Dan 2:44; 3:33; 6:27; 7:14, 18, 27.
2   Ps 93:1-2
3   Ps 47:1-3

As Creator, God's kingship is universal and eternal, and the basis on which God may justly assert sovereignty over all the kings of the earth and their respective deities.[1] Within this cosmic dominion, Israel is conceived of as a theocracy in a unique sense. By virtue of her covenant relationship with God,[2] Israel acknowledged Yahweh as her one true king. As Isaiah puts it:

> For the Lord is our judge,
> the Lord is our ruler,
> the Lord is our king,
> He will save us.[3]

> I am the Lord, your Holy One,
> the Creator of Israel,
> your king.[4]

The same thought is found elsewhere in the Old Testament.[5] So deep-seated indeed was the conviction that God alone was the rightful king of Israel that Samuel saw the demand for a human king as a rejection of Yahweh's divine kingship over Israel. 'The Lord said to Samuel, "Listen

---

1   For example Pss 2:1-11; 47:8; 95:3
2   It is perhaps worth observing that the Sinai covenant has many similarities to royal treaties in the ancient world, specifically suzerainty treaties between a Great King and his vassals. Although the nature and extent of the covenant/treaty parallel are sharply contested in current Old Testament studies, it is certainly the case that by means of the Sinai covenant Israel promised to be a loyal and obedient nation living directly under Yahweh's kingly rule and according to God's law.
3   Isa 33:22
4   Isa 43:15
5   For example, Ex 15:18; Isa 6:5; Jer 8:19; Mic 2:13; Zeph 3:15

to the voice of the people in all that they say to you; for they have not rejected you, but they have rejected me from being king over them"'.[1]

These two dimensions of Yahweh's present reign — God's reign over the whole of creation and God's reign over the people of Israel — may be related by saying that God reigns *by right* over heaven and earth, but that God's kingship exists in the human sphere *in fact* only where men and women willingly submit to God's rule. In the Old Testament period, Israel constituted the human community which sought to shape its life in response to God's kingly rule.

(b) Yahweh the Coming King

Despite the reality of Yahweh's present reign, the Old Testament writers recognise that all was still not right in the world. Most nations did not acknowledge Yahweh's lordship. Israel too often rebelled against it. Creation itself sometimes appeared out of control: floods, famine, death and disease seemed to defy God's perfect rule. And so the hope began to emerge that one day in the future God would come to establish his reign perfectly upon the earth, to reveal decisively his ruling arm against all that resisted it.

> Then the moon will be abashed and the sun ashamed,
> for the Lord of hosts will reign on Mount Zion and in Jerusalem.
> and before the elders he will manifest his glory.[2]

> Get you up to a high mountain, O Zion, herald of good tidings;
> lift up your voice with strength,

---

1   1 Sam 8:7; cf. 12:12
2   Isa 24:23

O Jerusalem, herald of good tidings,

lift it up, do not fear;

say to the cities of Judah,

"Here is your God!"

See the Lord God comes with might, and his arm rules for him;

his reward is with him and his recompense before him.[1]

An immense number of passages describe the character of the future kingdom of God,[2] with Second Isaiah being the greatest exponent of the theme. Beasley-Murray suggests that any summary of the nature of existence in the kingdom of God would have to include three main features:[3]

(i) The Universality of the Rule of Yahweh: In the future kingdom, Yahweh will rule as king over all the earth. Israel will give whole-hearted allegiance to God,[4] and all nations will be subject to God's reign.[5] Sometimes the submission of foreign nations to Israel, as well as to Yahweh, is depicted.[6] This universalist facet of eschatological hope is well summed up in the words of Zechariah: 'And the Lord will become

---

1   Isa 40:9ff
2   It should be said, of course, that the language of 'kingship' is not always used in depicting this impending state of affairs. Indeed kingdom *terminology* has a predominatnly present or historical orientation in the Old Testament. 'An eschatological dimension is present in Daniel and the prophets, but it is often not clearly defined, and is rarely spoken of explicitly as a kingdom', Selman, 'Kingdom of God', 189. Nonetheless, for our purposes the term 'kingdom of God' may still be used as a heuristic scheme for summing up all those expectations associated with the coming intervention of God to redeem his people and pacify creation.
3   G.R. Beasley-Murray, *Jesus and the Kingdom of God* (Grand Rapids: Eerdmans, 1986), 20
4   Isa 26:1-15; 28:5ff, 17ff; Ezek 11:17ff; 20:33ff; Hos 2:16f; Zech 8:1-8
5   Isa 25:6f; 45:1-22; 51:4f; 52:10f; 56:3f; Jer 3:17; Zeph 3:8f; Zech 8:20f; 14:9
6   Amos 9:11f; Mic 4:13; 7:8-17; Is 49:22-26; 60:4-16

king over all the earth. On that day the Lord will be one, and his name one' (14:9).

(ii) The Righteousness of the Kingdom: God will cleanse and renew the people of God.[1] The people of the kingdom shall be righteous and justice shall be secured for the oppressed.[2] A new covenant will be made with Israel.

> The days are surely coming, says the Lord, when I will make a new covenant with the house of Israel and the house of Judah. It will not be like the covenant that I made with their ancestors when I took them by the hand to bring them out of the land of Egypt — a covenant that they broke, though I was their husband, says the Lord. But this is the covenant that I will make with the house of Israel after those days, says the Lord: I will put my law within them, and I will write it on their hearts; and I will be their God, and they shall be my people.[3]

(iii) The Peace of the Kingdom: The term *shalom*, more than any other, captures the character of the eschatological hope of the Old Testament. *Shalom* is an all-embracing synonym for salvation,[4] and is perhaps best translated as 'wholeness', a condition of comprehensive 'all-righness'.[5] The peace of the future kingdom includes the absence of war;[6] the ending of infirmity and disease;[7] peace in humanity's relationship to God;[8] the

---

1   Isa 1:25f; 4:3f; 32:15f; Jer 31:31-33; Ezek 36:25f; Isa 52:13-52:12
2   Isa 11:3-5; 26:2; 28:5; 61:1-4
3   Jer 31:31-33
4   Isa 12; 21:17-24; 33:17ff; 41:21f; Jer 31:1-4; Hos 2:14f, 14:4f; Zeph 3:14-20
5   See Perry B. Yoder, *Shalom: The Bible's Word for Salvation, Justice and Peace* (Newton, KS: Faith & Life Press, 1987)
6   Isa 2:2f; 9:5f; Mic 5:4; Zech 9:9f
7   Isa 29:19; 35:5f; 42:7; 61:1ff
8   Isa 33:24; Jer 31:34; Mic 7:18; Hab 2:14

restoration of luxuriant fruitfulness in nature;[1] even the end of violence in the animal kingdom.[2] The 'peaceable kingdom' is evocatively pictured by the prophet Isaiah:

> The wolf shall live with the lamb,
> the leopard shall lie down with the kid,
> the calf and the lion and the fattling together,
> and a little child shall lead them.
> The cow and the bear shall graze,
> their young shall lie down together;
> and the lion shall eat straw like the ox.
> The nursing child shall play over the hole of the asp,
> and the weaned child shall put his hand on the adder's den.
> They will not hurt or destroy on all my holy mountain;
> for the earth will be full of the knowledge of the Lord
> as the waters cover the earth.[3]

Thus for the Old Testament writers, the goal of history will be reached in the revelation and universal acknowledgement of Yahweh's sovereignty, the triumph of God's justice and righteousness, and the establishment of peace and justice throughout the world. It should be noted that the prophetic hope in the Old Testament is a decidedly *earthly* hope, as Beasley-Murray stresses.

> When Yahweh comes to bring his kingdom, it is to this world that he comes and in this world that he establishes his reign. The hope of Israel is not for a home in heaven but for the revelation of the

---

1   Isa 35:1-10; 41:17f; Ezek 47; Hos 2:21-22; Joel 4:18; Am 9:13
2   Isa 11:6f, 35:9
3   Isa 11:6-9

glory of God in this world, when 'the earth shall be full of the glory of the Lord as the waters fill the sea' (Hab 2:14). As God's claim on man encompasses the totality of his life, so God's salvation for man encompasses the totality of human existence, including our historical existence.[1]

The relation of this expectation for the *eschatological kingdom* to *messianic expectation* in the Old Testament is an involved and contested issue. Suffice it to say that in some texts the Messiah is God's instrument to bring in the age of salvation,[2] while in others he is portrayed as the one to whom God will delegate the task of rule in the kingdom of God after the new order is established.[3] There can be little doubt, however, that in the minds of the populace the expectation for the coming of the Messiah would have strengthened and sharpened the hope for the coming of the reign of God.

First-Century Jewish Expectations

In the period after the writing of the last of the Old Testament books, the hope for the future age in which God would manifest his rule to bring peace and happiness continued as a major theme in Jewish eschatology. The actual expression 'the kingdom of God', or its equivalent in Matthew's Gospel, 'the kingdom of Heaven' (which means the kingdom of the One who is in Heaven, namely God), was not a common idiom,

---

1   Beasley-Murray, *Kingdom of God*, 25
2   For example, in Isa 42:1-4; 49:1-6; 50:4-9; 52:13-53:12
3   See, for example, Isa 9:1-7; 11:1-9; 40:9f; Mic 5:1-4; Jer 23:5f; Ezek 34:22-24; Zech 9:9f

partly because Jews of the time sought to avoid making direct utterances about God (even the term 'kingdom' could serve as a periphrasis for God). But the longing for a new age in which God's sovereignty would be revealed to the world was a widely cherished hope. This hope took on differing forms and shapes in the various streams of Jewish religious life. There was no orthodox or monolithic eschatological programme in Judaism to which every Jew subscribed; different sectors of the Jewish community nurtured differing understandings of what the coming reign of God might mean. Although vastly over-simplified and over-schematised, the following outline will serve to illustrate this diversity.

(i) Jewish Apocalypticism embraces an extraordinarily varied range of thought and literature, and it is not possible to identify within it a single normative 'doctrine' on the kingdom of God.[1] Dozens of apocalyptic documents were produced in the period 200 B.C.E. to 200 C.E., purporting to 'unveil' (the meaning of the Greek term *apocakalupsis*) divine secrets about the cosmos or the future world. This revelatory information was usually conveyed in highly symbolic, pictorial language, such as is found

---

1   There are several major works on apocalyptic, such as C. Rowland, *The Open Heaven* (London: SPCK, 1982), P.D. Hanson, *The Dawn of Apocalyptic* (Fortress: Philadelphia, 1979), and D.S. Russell, *Apocalyptic Ancient and Modern* (London: SCM, 1978). For much briefer, but still helpful, discussions, see R.J. Bauckham, 'The Rise of Apocalyptic', *Themelios* 3,2 (1978), 10-23; J.D.G. Dunn, *Unity and Diversity in the New Testament* (London:SCM, 1977), 309-316; N. Perrin, *The Kingdom of God in the Teaching of Jesus* (London: SCM, 1963), 160-185; Beasley-Murray, *Kingdom of God*, 39-62; C. Rowland, *Christian Origins* (London: SPCK, 1985), 56-64; J.H. Charlesworth, *Jesus Within Judaism* (London: SPCK, 1988), 33-42.

in the book of Daniel in the Old Testament and the book of Revelation in the New.[1]

Broadly speaking, apocalyptic thought is characterised by a combination of an incipient *cosmological dualism*, which sees the world in the grip of a cosmic conflict between two spirits, God and Satan (also called Beliar, Belial, Mastema, etc.), with a marked *temporal dualism* between 'this age' and 'the age to come'. The present age is full of affliction and sorrow, and largely given over to evil powers and political oppression. But these hostile forces shall be totally vanquished by the cataclysmic, violent intervention of God at the end of time to bring in his reign. As one apocalyptic prophet expresses it:

> But when Rome shall rule over Egypt as well, as she still hesitates to do, then the mightiest kingdom of the immortal king over us shall appear. And a holy prince shall come to wield the sceptre over all the world unto the ages of hurrying time.[2]

The advent of God's reign will bring destruction to the wicked, the resurrection of the righteous, and the complete transformation of creation. Paradise will be restored and the kingdom of God, where God's perfect will is done, will stand forever.

The relation of messianic hope to kingdom-expectation in apocalyptic literature is also quite diverse and unsystematic. In some apocalyptic writings a Messiah is not mentioned at all; in others his role is given little significance. Some documents anticipate a messianic kingdom as an

---

1   Other examples of apocalyptic or semi-apocalyptic writing in the Bible include
     Isa 24-27, Zech 9-14, Mark 13; 1 Thess 4:13-18; 2 Thess 2; 1-12 and 2 Pet 3:1-13
2   Sibyline Oracles 3:46f

interregnum before the full establishment of God's kingdom; in others, 'the Messiah is viewed as the form of Yahweh's presence in the kingdom'.[1]

(ii) The Qumran community was a kind of Jewish monastic group that lived on the western shores of the Dead Sea from sometime in the second century B.C.E. until it was wiped out by the Roman army marching to besiege Jerusalem in 68 C.E. The famed Dead Sea Scrolls, discovered in 1947, document the theology and communal life of this apocalyptic-priestly sect, which was almost certainly of Essene persuasion.[2] Founded by the Teacher of Righteousness, a priest who had seceded from the Jerusalem Temple, the community considered itself to be living at the end of the present age, the so-called 'epoch of wickedness'. The members of the community lived in ardent anticipation of the coming kingdom which would be a time of salvation, purification, peace and blessing.[3]

The Qumran sectarians considered themselves to be the people of the New Covenant, and seem to have believed that they were already, in some sense, participating in the blessings of the eschatological age. Even now they belonged to the heavenly Jerusalem and enjoyed the hidden paradise later to be revealed.[4] However they still looked to the future for the

---

1   Beasley-Murray, *Kingdom of God*, 62
2   Literature on the Qumran community is vast. Most recent New Testament
     Introductions include chapters on the community. See also the up-to-date
     discussions in G. Vermes, *The Dead Sea Scrolls in English* (Sheffield: JSOT,
     1987³), 1-57, and Charlesworth, *Jesus Within Judaism*, 54-76. On the
     kingdom-theme at Qumran, see B.T. Viviano, 'The Kingdom of God in Qumran
     Literature', in W Willis (ed.), *Kingdom of God*, 97-108.
3   Cf. 1QM 1:5; 17:7; 1QS 4:19-23
4   Cf. 1QH 6:24ff; 8:5ff

intervention of God to destroy the Gentile nations and secure the triumph of the sons of light.

(iii) Pharisaic Judaism centred around the Law, which was considered the means by which God's reign was present now in the world. By confessing allegiance to one God through the daily recitation of the *Shema* (cf. Deut 6:4) and living in obedience to the Torah, especially its prescriptions for ritual purity, one could 'take upon oneself the yoke of the kingdom of heaven' — in other words, live under the kingly rule of God.[1] Yet Pharisaic Judaism also nursed the hope for the eschatological consummation of God's current reign. This indeed was the object of regular prayers at the time of Jesus. In the *Tefillah* or prayer of the *Eighteen Benedictions,* recited three times a day by pious Jews, supplication is made for the coming of the kingdom.

> Blow the great horn of our liberation, and lift a banner to gather our exiles. . . Restore our judges as at the first, and our counsellors as at the beginning; and reign Thou over us, Thou alone. . .Be merciful, O Lord our God, in thy great mercy, towards Israel thy people, and towards thy temple and thy habitation, and towards the kingdom of the house of David, thy righteous one.

Similarly in the *Kaddish*, the ancient Aramaic doxology used to close synagogue worship in Jesus' day, the aspiration for the future kingdom is evident:

> Magnified and sanctified be his great name
> in the world which he has created according to his will.

---

1   Cf. Jesus' saying in Matt 11:29f

> May he establish his kingdom in your lifetime and in your days,
> and in the lifetime of all the house of Israel,
> even speedily and at a near time.
> And to this day. Amen.

The establishment of the eschatological kingdom was something God alone could do. Nevertheless the rabbis held that humans were able to influence the coming of God's kingdom through the power of repentance. If Israel would repent and keep the Law perfectly, the kingdom would come.

(iv) The Targumic conception of the kingdom of God has received particular attention in recent scholarship. The Targums are mainly Aramaic paraphrases of the Hebrew scriptures. Unlike other intertestamental literature, the motif of the kingdom of God in these writings has a fixed, standard meaning, and one that is different from the rabbinic use of 'the kingdom of heaven' for the rule of the Law. According to Bruce Chilton, a scholar who has devoted much attention to this theme, it denotes the self-disclosure of God, the Lord revealing himself in strength on behalf of his people. 'The emphasis is on the dynamic, personal presence of God — not on the nature of God in itself, but on his saving, usually future, activity'.[1] In Targumic theology, the future revelation of

---

1   B.D. Chilton, 'Introduction', in B.D. Chilton (ed.) *The Kingdom of God* (London: SPCK, 1985), 22; cf. also his essay 'God in Strength' in the same volume, 121-32. See also his article 'Regnum Dei Deus Est', *Scottish Journal of Theology* 31 (1978), 261-70; his full-scale treatment, *God in Strength: Jesus' Announcement of the Kingdom* (Linz: Plochl, Freistadt, 1979); and his more general *A Galilean Rabbi and His Bible* (Wilmington: Michael Glazier, 1984).

the kingdom is particularly associated with Mount Zion, and there is a developed interest in the Davidic Messiah.

(v) The term *Zealot* is traditionally applied to Jewish extremists who were not content to wait quietly for God to bring in his kingdom but wished to hasten its coming with the sword.[1] The Zealots were not so much a single, clearly defined party, like the Pharisees or Sadducees, but more a general freedom movement unified by a common ideology of militant defence of the faith. The movement apparently had its origins in the resistance to Roman taxation led by Judas the Galilean in 6 B.C.E., and according to the first-century Jewish historian Flavius Josephus, the Zealots were the dominant force in the revolt against Rome in 66-70 B.C.E. Several made their heroic last stand in the fortress of Masada in 73 C.E.

Stressing that God alone was the rightful king of Israel, and seeing all co-operation with Rome as treachery against God's rule, Zealots advocated violent opposition to the pagan occupying power. They perhaps hoped this would ignite a messianic war in which God would intervene to vanquish the Roman empire and vindicate his rightful sovereignty. According to the Zealots,

> The eschatological liberation of Israel, the great hope of Palestinian Judaism in the century before and the century after Christ, could not become a reality if pious folks waited passively for the reign of God to break in, but only if they worked actively for its realization.

---

1   The definitive work on the Zealots is M. Hengel, *The Zealots* (Edinburgh: T & T Clark, 1989). The kingdom-concept of the Zealots is accented by J. Riches, *Jesus and the Transformation of Judaism* (London: Darton, Longman & Todd, 1980), 93ff.

This took place through 'zeal for the Law,' i.e., through the armed battle against the pagans who were without the Law and the Jews who violated the Law. Included in this latter category were all who submitted to the Roman yoke.[1]

The revolutionary strategy of the Zealot movement was thus religiously motivated. It was fuelled by a near fanatical devotion to the Second Commandment — 'You shall have no other gods before me'. Loyalty to God's kingdom, and any form obedience to Rome, were mutually exclusive commitments.

(vi) The perspective of the *Sadducees* was rather different. Whereas the Essenes, Pharisees and Zealots may be understood as renewal movements in Judaism, the Sadducees were more concerned with preserving the status quo. Comprising chief priests, aristocrats and wealthy landlords, the Sadducees exercised religious, political and economic power in the Jewish community. They stressed co-operation with, rather than opposition to, Rome; it was in their own best interests to do so! Theologically the Sadducees were arch-conservatives. They accorded authority to the written Law alone and opposed the oral interpretations elaborated by the Pharisees. They rejected speculations about angels and demons, and such novel doctrines as resurrection of the dead.[2] Their corporate eschatology was also distinctive, as Longenecker explains.

---

1   M. Hengel, *Was Jesus a Revolutionist?* (Philadelphia: Fortress Press, 1971), 11.
2   Cf. Mark 12:18-27

The Sadducees were descendants of the Hasmoneans, who looked back to Mattathias, Judas, Jonathan, and Simon (168-134 BC) as having inaugurated the Messianic Age (cf. Jub 23:23-30; 31:9-20; 1 Macc 14:4-15,41) and saw themselves as perpetuating what their Fathers had begun. . .They rejected what they considered to be vain hopes for God's heavenly intervention in the life of the nation and for a coming Messiah, since, as they believed, the age of God's promise had begun with the Maccabean heroes and was continuing on under their supervision. For them, the Messiah was an ideal, not a person, and the Messianic Age was a process, not a cataclysmic or even datable event.[1]

Such a view of the kingdom constituted a convenient theological justification for the retention of power, of an increasingly predatory kind, by the Establishment-elite in Judea. Few people outside of Saducean ranks would have shared it.

(vii) Mention should finally be made of the first-century Jewish prophet, *John the Baptist,* who, according to Matthew, publicly proclaimed the imminence of God's kingdom.[2] It is clear from the Gospel reports that John closely linked the coming of God's kingdom with the appearance of a messianic figure, 'the Mightier One', who would carry out the double task of judgment (immersion in fire), and salvation (immersion in the eschatological Spirit).[3] In contrast to the Zealots, but

---

1   R.N. Longenecker, 'The Acts of the Apostles', in F.E. Gaebelein (ed.), *The Expositor's Bible Commentary* (Grand Rapids: Zondervan, 1981), IX. 301.
2   Matt 3:1f. For a helpful introduction to John the Baptist's ministry, with suggestions for further reading, see G.N. Stanton, *The Gospels and Jesus* (Oxford: OUP 1989), 165-176.
3   Mark 1:1-6/Matt 3:1-12/Lk 3:1-9, 15-17; Jn 1:19-28

in keeping with Jesus, John's conception of the coming kingdom transcended Jewish particularism; radical obedience to the Jewish Torah was not, for John, the sole criterion of judgment. The approaching kingdom demanded a response of repentance by everyone, Jews from all walks of life and even Roman soldiers. The immense popularity of John with the ordinary people of Palestine is a significant gauge of how vibrant the hope for the intervention of God's rule was at the time of Jesus.

Summary

The biblical affirmation of God's eternal kingship and the expectation for its ultimate visible manifestation upon the earth was thus nurtured and developed in varying forms in early Judaism. There was no normative doctrine of the kingdom of God to which all pious Jews subscribed. But behind the diversity of expression certain common features are discernible.

To begin with, Jewish attitudes to the kingdom were essentially *forward-looking*. Every Jew knew that God reigned eternally in the heavens and was the rightful king of Israel. But, with the possible exception of some in Sadduccean circles, most Jews recognised that the effective reign of God was something hoped for rather than experienced in full. History would only reach its divinely-intended goal when God appeared at the end of the age to vindicate divine sovereignty in face of all that defied it on earth.

Hand-in-hand with the longing for the kingdom went the expectation for a human or super-human deliverer, a *messianic personage*, who would play some decisive role in establishing the kingdom or ruling in it as God's representative. His appearance would entail the restoration of the Jewish nation and the end of foreign domination. 'The common denominator of all eschatological formulations of the kingdom', observes John Collins, 'in addition to the postulate of divine sovereignty, was rejection of foreign rule. The implementation of the kingdom of God, whether by a messiah or a direct heavenly intervention, implied the destruction of the kings and the mighty of this world.' [1]

But fundamental to Old Testament-Jewish eschatology was the august idea of *the coming of God in person* to reign as sovereign, the living God present and powerful upon the earth.[2] The hope for the kingdom was essentially the hope for a definitive and permanent theophany, the tangible appearance of God to abolish evil, establish righteousness in the world, and bring creation to its goal and fulfilment.

---

1   J.J. Collins, 'The Kingdom of God in the Apocrypha and Pseudepigrapha', in W. Willis (ed.), *Kingdom of God*, 95. 'In general terms', says E.P. Sanders, 'it may be said that "Jewish eschatology" and "the restoration of Israel" are almost synonymous", *Jesus and Judaism* (London: SCM, 1985), 97.

2   So, e.g., C.H. Dodd, *The Founder of Christianity* (London: Collins, 1977), 93f; E. Jenni, 'Eschatology of the Old Testament', *Interpreter's Dictionary of the Bible*, Vol 2, 127f; Chilton concludes that in the Targumim, 'the kingdom of God refers to God himself, as it were personally,' 'Regnum Dei', 266. One of the great merits of Beasley-Murray's recent book, is the close connection he demonstrates between Old Testament traditions relating to theophany, the Day of Yahweh, and the coming of the kingdom. They all centre on the coming of God to abolish evil and set up God's perfect order.

3

The Proclamation of Jesus

*T*he mood then of the Jewish people in first-century Palestine seems to have been one of expectancy. They lived in a time of political oppression and they ached for God to do something about it. They recalled past experiences of divine intervention in their history and, despite frequent disappointment, they believed God would intervene again soon. Then one day, 'after John was arrested, Jesus came into Galilee, preaching the good news of God and saying, "The time is fulfilled, and the kingdom of God has come near; repent and believe in the good news"'.[1] The time of waiting was over; the time of fulfilment had arrived!

We have already noted how Jesus presupposed his hearers would understand what he meant by the phrase 'kingdom of God', so that he never needed to define it. At the same time, he devoted much effort to explaining what he considered to be the nature and implications of God's kingdom; he would begin many of his parables with some such expression as 'the kingdom of God may be compared to.'[2] In other words, Jesus used the traditional concept of God's kingdom as a point of contact with his audience, but went on to invest the expression with his own distinctive configuration of ideas and emphases. As John Riches helpfully explains it, Jesus took over an existing term and, while retaining its essential or core meaning, purged it of some of its conventional associations and substituted others.[3]

---

1   Mark 1:14f, cf. Matt 1:17
2   Mark 4:26; 4:30/Matt 13:31/Luke 13:18; Matt 13:24; 13:33/Luke 13:20;
     Matt13:44, 45, 47; 18:23; 20:1; 22:2; 25:1
3   J. Riches, *Jesus and the Transformation of Judaism* (London: Darton, Longman
     & Todd, 1980), 87-111

It is generally agreed today that the core meaning of the kingdom of God in Jesus' teaching is the idea of *God exercising ruling power*. The emphasis falls principally on the reign or redemptive sovereignty of God rather than on the domain or realm over which God rules. Because the English noun 'kingdom' evokes the passive idea of a territory ruled by a monarch (for example, the 'United Kingdom'), many prefer to translate the Greek word *basileia* in the Gospels as 'reign' or 'rule' so as to convey the dynamic thrust of the concept.

This is quite valid. But we should beware of too sharply contrasting, as some scholars do, the notions of reign and realm.[1] Not only does the ruling activity of a monarch necessarily create a realm or sphere — be it geographical, temporal or spiritual — in which that reign is an effective reality, but there are also many places in the Gospels where *basileia* signifies the sphere of God's rule, such as in the sayings about 'entering' the kingdom.[2] In such cases the word 'kingdom' is a good translation, as long as we bear in mind that even here the term denotes not a static locality to be entered but a dynamic event to be experienced.[3]

Nonetheless the important thing to note in this connection is that in Jesus' preaching, the 'kingdom of God' is primarily something *God* does, and only secondarily, as a corollary of this, the sphere in which this is

---

1   See the discussions in S. Aalen, '"Reign" and "House" in the kingdom of God in the Gospels", *New Testament Studies* 8 (1961/2), 215-240; G.E. Ladd, 'The Kingdom of God - Reign or Realm?', *Journal of Biblical Literature* 81 (1962), 230-238.

2   For example, Mark 9:47/Matt 19:88; Mark 10:15/Matt 18:3/Luke 18:7 (cf. John 3:5); Mark 10:23-25/Matt 19:23f/Luke 18:24f; Matt 5:20; 7:21; 8:11f; 21:31; 23:13/Luke 11:52

3   See J. Marcus, 'Entering into the Kingly Power of God', *Journal of Biblical Literature* 107, 4 (1988), 663-75

experienced and accepted. *The kingdom of God denotes the governing activity of God as ruler; the time and sphere in which God's kingly power and will hold sway.*

This much would have been generally intelligible to Jesus' first hearers. But Jesus brought this idea of God's saving sovereignty into connection with a number of distinctive associations. Here I want to touch briefly on some of the distinctive contours of Jesus' kingdom conception, and in the next chapter outline three major dimensions of his ministry the term embraces.

Before doing so, a word of caution is in order. Out of a quite natural, and legitimate, concern to preserve the unique significance of Jesus' person and work, Christian scholarship has always tried to identify or highlight those features of Jesus' teaching and conduct that were unique to him, the concerns and emphases that set him apart from his Jewish contemporaries. Much insight into the historical Jesus has been gained from this endeavour, but often at the price of Jesus' own authentic *Jewishness.* In the past, critical scholarship, employing the so-called 'criterion of dissimilarity' to identify historically reliable material in the Gospels,[1] has virtually fabricated a *Gentile Jesus,* a first-century Palestinian Jew totally out of place in the Palestinian Judaism of his day and at odds with the Palestinian Jewish Jesus-movement that followed after his time! Fortunately this travesty of historical scholarship is

---

1   This critical canon maintains that one can only be sure that sayings ascribed to Jesus in the Gospels are authentic (that is, actually uttered by Jesus) when they cannot be paralleled in either contemporary Jewish tradition or in later Christian tradition; only what is utterly unique to Jesus can be accepted with confidence as authentic.

increasingly giving way to a desire to understand Jesus *within* the Judaism of his time, to recover Jesus the Jew.[1]

This means that in discussing the characteristic outlook of Jesus, we must not exaggerate its uniqueness. Items in Jesus' teaching that have in the past been hailed as unparalleled in contemporary Judaism have frequently been found, through subsequent research, to be typically Jewish. Oftentimes in his teaching Jesus was simply echoing and endorsing well-known Jewish themes (not least Old Testament themes!) or giving special weight to neglected or minor aspects in Jewish wisdom. Certainly, as we will see, there are features in Jesus' instruction that *are* original and unique to him. But the significance of Jesus' teaching does not just lie in its unprecedented features; it lies primarily in the way he brought together widely scattered aspects of Old Testament-Jewish thought into a distinctive configuration, to describe life under the reign of God. In other words, the uniqueness of Jesus resides in the *total shape of his ministry and in the mystery of his own person,* not in the fact that he said things no one had ever said before (although on occasions he did that as well).

In what follows, several features of Jesus' message about the kingdom of God are described as 'characteristic' or 'distinctive'. Not all these things can be said to be utterly unique to Jesus; but they are still distinctive of him. They are distinctive in the sense that they are distinguishing marks of Jesus' outlook and message. Some of these were familiar Jewish beliefs

---

1   Representative of this concern are such works as G. Vermes, *Jesus the Jew* (London: SCM, 1983[2]); E.P. Sanders, *Jesus and Judaism* (London: SCM, 1985); and J.H. Charlesworth, *Jesus Within Judaism* (London: SPCK, 1988)

or concerns that acquired special, and sometimes dramatically new, significance by the particular context, emphasis or interpretation Jesus gave them. With this mind, we turn now to four distinguishing themes in Jesus' proclamation of the kingdom of God.

The Presence of the Kingdom

Jewish eschatology looked towards an unmistakable manifestation of God's ruling power at the end of present history. God's control of things at present was to some degree hidden and open to contradiction; but the future would see the incontrovertible triumph of this rule.

Jesus agreed that the final triumph of God was still to come.[1] He taught his followers to pray 'your kingdom come, your will be done on earth as it is in heaven'. But he also dared to suggest that God's future victory was *even now* manifesting itself in human affairs. The kingly reign of God was *already* operative in present history. Future hope had become present experience. Many actions of Jesus and several of his sayings make this clear.[2] As one example we may quote Luke 17:20f:

---

1   For example, Matt 6:10/Luke 11:2; Matt 8:11f/Luke 13:28f; Mark 9:1/Matt
     16:29/Luke 9:27[?]; Mark 14:25/Matt 26:29/Luke 22:18; Mark 13-24-27/Matt
     24:29-31/Luke 21:25-28; Luke 17:20-37; 19:11ff
2   See for example, Mark 1:14f/Matt 4:17; Mark 4:11/Matt 13:11/Luke 8:10; Matt
     11:26/Luke 7:22-23; Matt 12:28/Luke 11:20; Matt 13:16-17/Luke 10:23f; Luke
     4:16-30; 16:16.

Once Jesus was asked by the Pharisees when the kingdom was coming, and he answered, 'The kingdom of God is not coming with things that can be observed; nor will they say, "Look here it is!" or "There it is!" For, in fact, the kingdom of God is among you' (*entos humin*).[1]

The crucial thing to grasp in this connection is that when Jesus declared the presence of the kingdom, he was not referring merely to the eternal reign of God in the heavens. He was instead proclaiming the *present assertion of God's end-time rule*, the current manifestation of God's future saving sovereignty. Simply to assert that God was ruling in the present time as king would be a Jewish commonplace. But to claim that the kingdom promised for the end of time was now present and operative seems to have been a bold innovation.[2] 'He is the only Jew of ancient times known to us,' explains the Jewish scholar David Flusser, 'who preached

---

1   The proper translation of the Greek phrase *entos humin* is controverted matter. Most scholars accept 'in your midst' or 'among you' as conveying Jesus' intention. See the discussion in the commentaries, especially those by I.H. Marshall, *The Gospel of Luke* (Exeter: Paternoster, 1978), 655, and J.A. Fitzmyer, *The Gospel According to Luke* (Garden City, New York: Doubleday, 1985), II.1161f.

2   Some scholars believe that a similar juxtaposition of present and future notions of the eschatological kingdom existed at Qumran, although other experts dispute this. It should be noted, however, that any sense of the *presence* of salvation at Qumran was closely bound up with the cultic nature of the community. This was not the case with Jesus. See Beasley-Murray's review of the evidence, *Jesus and the Kingdom of God* (Grand Rapids: Eerdmans, 1986), 46-51. Still a very useful discussion of the present-future dimensions of Jesus' kingdom concept is W.G. Kümmel, *Promise and Fulfilment: The Eschatological Message of Jesus* (London: SCM, 1957). See also G.E. Ladd, *The Presence of the Future: The Eschatology of Biblical Realism* (Grand Rapids: Eerdmans, 1974)

not only that men were on the threshold of the end of time, but that the new age of salvation had already begun.'[1]

Space does not permit a discussion of the involved debate in scholarly circles this century between advocates of 'consistent', 'realised' and 'inaugurated' eschatology.[2] Suffice to say that the first interpretation holds that Jesus thought the coming of the kingdom to be an entirely future, though imminent, event. The second approach insists that he considered the kingdom to have already come in all its fullness in his own ministry, with little more to follow. The third maintains that whilst Jesus saw the final consummation of the kingdom to be still outstanding, he announced that this future state of affairs was being inaugurated in his mission. It is this third interpretation that has won the scholarly consensus. Jesus proclaimed *both* that the kingdom had already come *and* that it was still to come in its entirety. His kingdom message (and indeed the whole of New Testament theology) is pervaded by this distinctive 'already...not yet' tension. He taught his followers to pray for the *coming* of the kingdom,[3] yet also to celebrate its *presence* among them in his own person and work.[4]

---

1   David Flusser, *Jesus* (New York: Herder & Herder, 1969), 85. For a review of
      the attitude of Jewish scholars to Jesus' kingdom proclamation, see D.A. Hagner
      The Jewish Reclamation of Jesus (Grand Rapids: Zondervan, 1984), 133-90.
2   For a convenient review, see W. Willis (ed.), *The Kingdom of God in
      20th-Century Interpretation* (Peabody, MA: Hendrickson, 1987), 1-65
3   Matt 6:10/Luke 11:2
4   Cf. Mark 2:18-20; Matt 11:16-19/Luke 7:31-35

The Hiddeness of the Kingdom

I once heard a Jewish rabbi say that the reason why he did not accept Jesus as the Messiah is because the kingdom had still not come. This (understandable) reaction brings into focus a second distinguishing feature of Jesus' kingdom message — the concealment of the present kingdom in history.

When Jesus proclaimed the presence of the kingdom, he was not saying that the end of the world had come. Rather he was saying that the *God of the end of the world* had come, in an unprecedented way, exerting eschatological might to initiate the age of salvation, to commence the chain of events that would culminate in a transformed universe. In other words, the promise of the kingdom was being fulfilled in an unexpected manner — not initially as the visible, public act of sovereignty by God to set up the divine reign on earth, as popularly expected, but as a secret or hidden invasion of divine power in the on-going flow of human affairs.

Indeed the future kingdom had begun its existence in such an inauspicious and unimpressive manner that it could easily be missed by the spiritually undiscerning. This is probably what Jesus meant by the 'secret' or 'mystery' of the kingdom discernible only by the eyes of faith.[1] The end-time rule of God was secretly, though powerfully, at work in present circumstances, in advance of its future revelation.

Of course, in one way the evidence and effects of the presence of the kingdom were everywhere apparent. The healings and exorcisms, the

---

1   Mark 4:11/Matt 13:11/Luke 8:10

feeding miracles and table communion with outcasts, the forgiveness of sins and the restoration of the lost to fellowship with God, the deeds and words that 'fulfilled' the Law and the Prophets, the creation of a messianic community to live a new lifestyle according to eschatological values — all these features of Jesus' ministry functioned as 'signs' or evidence of the dawning of a new age.

But the Gospels make it abundantly clear that the signs were inherently *ambiguous*. Those with eyes to see and ears to hear could recognise in them the manifestation of God's reign. But the spiritually unperceptive, and those who deliberately hardened their hearts in unbelief, could explain them otherwise. They might be taken as evidence of madness[1] or demonic possession.[2] They could be seen as the works of just another prophet like John the Baptist[3] or even of a false prophet.[4] They could be dismissed as the self-inflated posturings of a man of common origins.[5] In the final instance, they could be construed as blasphemies against God.[6] This ambiguity is part and parcel of the veiled manifestation of the kingdom of God in the ministry of Jesus.

The theme of many of the so-called parables of growth[7] is that the present and future dimensions of the in-breaking kingdom are related to one another as seedtime is to harvest. Just as a harvest begins

---

1   Mark 3:21
2   Mark 3:22-30/Matt 12:22-27/Luke 11:14-23; John 8:48
3   Mark 6:14f/Matt 16:14f/Luke 9:7f; Mark 8:27-8/Matt 16:13f/Luke 9:18f
4   Cf. Mark 13:6, 22/Matt 24:5f, 23-26/Luke 21:8; Mark 15:29-32/Matt
     27:39-44/Luke 23:35-37; Matt 7:21-23. On the possibility of Jesus' works being
     understood as evidence he was a false prophet, see C. Brown, *History and Faith:
     A Personal Explanation* (Leicester: IVP, 1987), 78-85
5   Mark 6:1-6/Matt 13:53-58
6   Mark 2:7/Matt 9:3/Luke 5:21; Mark 14:63-65/Matt 26:59-65
7   For example, Mark 4:26-29; 30-32/Matt 13:31-33/Luke 13:18-21

unobstrusively with a seed buried in the ground, so the eschatological harvest of the kingdom has begun in the ministry of Jesus as a transforming power concealed, or 'buried' as it were, in the midst of everyday events. Despite its unassuming proportions and the resistance and rejection it encounters, the present manifestation of God's rule is the springboard of the future, from which, in time, God will manifest universal dominion.

The Inclusiveness and Peace of the Kingdom

A third important contour of Jesus' kingdom message is the way he systematically purged the Jewish eschatological expectation of its nationalistic and its militaristic connotations. Both these features find clear expression in the Psalms of Solomon 17, a Jewish document dating from near the time of Jesus.

> Behold, O Lord, raise up unto them their king, the son of David, in the time in which you see, O God, that he may reign over Israel your servant. Gird him with strength, that he may shatter unrighteous rulers and that he may purge Jerusalem from nations that trample her down to destruction. Wisely, righteously, he shall thrust out sinners from the inheritance. He shall destroy the pride of the sinner as a potter's vessel. With a rod of iron he shall break in pieces all their substance. He shall destroy the godless nations with the word of his mouth. At his rebuke nations shall flee before him, and he shall reprove sinners for the thoughts of their hearts. He shall gather together a holy people, whom he shall lead in righteousness, and he shall judge the tribes of the people that has been sanctified by the Lord his God. He shall not suffer unrighteousness to lodge any more in their midst, nor shall there dwell with them any man that knows wickedness. For he shall know them, that they are all sons of their God (17:23-30).

This expresses the popular hope[1] that God would manifest his ruling power by raising up a warrior king, a messianic son of David, who would crush Israel's enemies and restore the nation's independence under God and her primacy among the nations of the world. The universalist elements in Old Testament prophecy, which speak of the Gentiles also participating in eschatological salvation, tended to be understood in Jesus' day as foreshadowing the subjugation of the nations to Israelite hegemony in the kingdom of God.

Even the expectation of the Qumran separatists was a decidedly national-military one. The people of Qumran were preparing to be the army of the Lord, whom God would use as instruments of his annihilation of the wicked — Romans, Gentiles, and apostate Jews alike — and usher in, under the Messiahs of Aaron and Israel, the promised kingdom.[2] 'The Qumran kingdom vision is...national rather than universal in its aims; militaristic, vindictive, violent, and somewhat more deterministic in its means, with no hint of love of enemies or forgiveness of sins.'[3]

Now there is not a trace of such a conception in the teaching of Jesus. We could say that, in general terms, Jesus transformed such exclusivistic and martial expectations in three major ways.

(i) He drew attention to the *inclusive* (or international) more than the *exclusive* (or national) dimensions of the kingdom. True, Jesus historically directed his mission to 'the lost sheep of the house of Israel,'[4] and

---

1   On this, see G. Vermes, *Jesus*, 130ff
2   Beasley-Murray, *Kingdom of God*, 208
3   B.T. Viviano, 'The Kingdom of God in the Qumran Literature', in Willis, *Kingdom of God*, 107
4   Matt 15:24; cf. 10:5f

summoned twelve disciples to symbolise his claim upon the whole nation.[1] Certainly, as current scholarship stresses, Jesus was pre-eminently concerned with the eschatological restoration of Israel as the covenant people of God. But this mission-priority does not express a xenophobia or nationalistic chauvinism on his part.

Jesus did not confine his ministry exclusively to Jews but also related freely to Gentiles.[2] He once praised a Roman centurion — a military leader of the unclean occupying power — for having greater faith than ever he found in Israel.[3] According to the synoptic writers, Jesus even looked ahead to the time when his followers would proclaim the kingdom of God throughout the Gentile world.[4]

Furthermore, Jesus never regarded the kingdom as an automatic blessing for Israel, or even for her most righteous members. Inheritance of the kingdom was by invitation; it was a gift offered by God to the nation that had to be received by repentance and faith.[5] If Israel's leaders refused to accept the offer, Jesus declared, 'the kingdom of God will be taken away from you and given to a people that produces the fruit of the kingdom'.[6] In such an event, 'the sons of the kingdom will be thrown into outer darkness', and in their place 'many will come from east and west and will eat with Abraham and Isaac and Jacob in the kingdom of heaven'.[7] The

---

1   Cf. Matt 19:28/Luke 22:29f
2   For example, Mark 5:1-20/Matt 8:28-34/Luke 8:26-39; Mark 7:24-30/Matt
     15:21-28; Matt 8:5-13/Luke 7:1-10; John 4:43-54
3   Matt 8:10/Luke 7:9
4   For example, Mark 13:10/Matt 24:13; 28:19f; cf. Acts 1:8
5   For example, Mark 1:15/Matt 4:17; Mark 10:15/Matt 18:3/Luke 18:17; Matt
     7:21ff; 21:31, 36
6   Matt 21:43/Luke 20:16
7   Matt 8:11f/Luke 13:28f

horror of this scenario for Jesus' hearers is difficult for us to imagine.[1] The suggestion that national Israel might be excluded from her own promised destiny and that the privileges that should be hers would be conferred on the Gentile nations, 'marks Jesus off from every contemporary Jewish preacher in his native land other than John the Baptist.'[2]

The summoning of the twelve disciples served not only as a symbolic expression of Jesus' appeal to the Jewish nation. It also symbolised the foundation of a new kind of Israel, an international community of salvation comprising all who responded to the gospel of the kingdom in repentance and faith. Put another way, Jesus' ultimate aim was to recreate Israel in the image of the eschatological kingdom.[3] He called Israel to become an inclusive community that opened its doors to all — Jew and Gentile, male and female, rich and poor, godly and godless — who embraced the rule of God revealed in his own person and ministry. 'Do not be afraid little flock,' Jesus said to the nucleus of this new community, 'for it is your Father's good pleasure to give you the kingdom'.[4]

(ii) Another way Jesus transformed nationalist expectation was by *targeting the real enemy.* The power that needed to be overthrown to usher

---

1 Cf. Luke 4:24-30
2 Beasley-Murray, *Kingdom of God,* 91 (commenting on Luke 4:25-27). See also his exegesis on Matt 8:11f on 172ff
3 J. Ramsey Michaels criticises Christian scholarship for minimizing the Jewishness of Jesus' vision of the kingdom of God and insits that Jesus was 'an apocalyptic prophet of the restoraction of Israel' whose expectation centred 'not on the whole world, but on Jerusalem and the nation of Israel' (115). However, as Michaels himself observes, the parables portray a radical change to existing conceptions of the saved community. 'If Jesus heralded a restored Israel, he heralded also a transformed, a topsy-turvy Israel, for he came, as he said, "not to call the righteous, but sinners" (Mark 2:17),' 'The Kingdom of God and the Historical Jesus', in Willis, *Kingdom of God,* 116.
4 Luke 12:32

in the kingdom was not the legions of Rome but the legions of Satan.[1] Satan is the great usurper[2] whose *basileia* stands opposed to God's.[3] Satan is the 'strong man' who must be bound before his house can be plundered.[4] It was Satan, not Caesar, that Jesus had to contend with at the outset of his public ministry and repeatedly throughout its course.[5] And it was Satan who stood behind the political events leading up to the passion and death of Jesus.[6] For Jesus then, the kingly power of God was operative not to crush Israel's Gentile enemies but to shatter the demonic powers that enslaved humanity and caused so much suffering and wickedness.

(iii) Thirdly, Jesus *utterly repudiated violence and military insurrection* as a fitting means for promoting the kingdom. For Jesus, the peaceable kingdom of Old Testament hope could not be realised by the edge of the sword.[7] On the contrary, the approach of God's kingdom brought with it a radically new demand: 'love your enemies and pray for those who persecute you, so that you may be children of your Father in heaven'.[8]

Members of the kingdom community are to be peacemakers.[9] They are not to live by the principle of an eye for an eye and a tooth for a tooth, nor

---

1   Mark 5:9/Luke 8:30
2   Cf. Matt 13:19, 38f
3   Mark 3:24/Matt 12:25/Luke 11:18
4   Mark 3:27/Matt 12:29/Luke 11:21-23
5   Mark 1:12f; Matt 4:1-11/Luke 3:1-13; cf. Luke 10:18
6   Luke 22:3; John 13:2, 27
7   See A. Trocmé, *Jesus and the Nonviolent Revolution* (Scottdale: Herald Press, 1973); M. Hengel, *Victory Over Violence* (London: SPCK, 1975)
8   Matt 5:44f
9   Matt 5:9

to resist evil by evil means.[1] Rather they are to turn the other cheek to the aggressor, to give freely to the confiscator, and to transform duties of compulsion into loving service of the oppressor.[2] 'This aspect of Jesus' thought', observes Charlesworth, 'is the most distinctive or unique aspect of his ethical teachings. As far as we know, no other Jew, or Jewish group, drew that extreme inference from the relevant ethical passages in the Old Testament'.[3]

This radical emphasis on enemy-loving not only sets Jesus apart from all other Jewish teachers of his day; it is, according to Jesus himself, one of the decisive differences between the *modus operandi* of God's kingdom and the kingdoms of this world. Jesus regarded the suggestion that he resort to violent means to achieve his goals as Satanic temptation,[4] and he severely reprimanded his disciples when they sought to use force to punish those who failed to offer them hospitality[5] or to protect him from physical harm.[6] At his trial before Pilate, Jesus cited the fact that his followers did not wage war as evidence that his kingdom did not conform to the kingdoms of this world.[7]

Clearly then Jesus thoroughly reinterpreted the nationalistic-militaristic hopes of the Old Testament and later Jewish

---

1   On this translation of the Greek text of Matt 5:39, *to ponero* is understood as instrumental. This coheres well with the way the later New Testament writers understood this saying (cf. Rom 12:17, 19-21; 13:8-10; 1 Pet 3:9; 1 Thess 5:15). On this and the whole subject of the Bible and war, see W.M. Swartley, *Slavery Sabbath, War and Women* (Scottdale: Herald Press, 1982), 96-149
2   Matt 5:38-48
3   Charlesworth, *Jesus within Judaism*, 38. This pointed is conceded by many Jewish scholars; see Hagner, *Jewish Reclamation*, 144-50
4   Cf. Matt 5:8-10 and 16:21-23
5   Luke 9:51-56
6   Luke 22:49-51/Matt 26:52/John 18:11; cf. Luke 22:38
7   John 18:36

literature in the direction of a spiritual liberation which was independent of, and in some senses even set against, Israel's national fortunes. This is certainly not to say that Jesus proclaimed a *purely spiritual* kingdom unrelated to the concrete issues of social and political life. Haughey is right to reject this view as a caricature of Jesus' teaching:

> While the kingdom preached by Jesus is purified by him and transcends the socio-political realities of this world, it was never meant to leave these or disdain them or prescind from them. Even though some portion of the population of Jesus' contemporaries riveted their expectations to the intra-mundane, it was the confinement of their expectations to the intra-mundane that Jesus railed against, not the socio-political framework of these expectations. It would seem a cruel-trick if the long awaited Messiah had a wholly other-world, 'the next life,' in mind when every expectation entertained by Israel was social and national in character, since this was what their Scriptures had taught them to believe.[1]

As we will see later, Jesus' conception of the kingdom included a implicit strategy for the transformation of social life, based on the prophetic denunciation of violence and injustice on the one hand and the creation of an alternative human society seeking to live according to the standards and values of the coming new age, on the other. In no sense did Jesus repudiate the social realism of his Jewish heritage.

---

1.   John C. Haughey, S.J. 'Jesus as the Justice of God', in John C. Haughey (ed.), *The Faith That Does Justice: Examining the Christian Sources for Social Change* (New York/Ramsey/Toronto: Paulist Press, 1977), 268

The Christological Focus of the Kingdom

A fourth crucial ingredient in Jesus' kingdom message was the *central role he ascribed to himself* in relation to the kingdom, in both its present and future dimensions.

In Old Testament-Jewish tradition, as we have seen, the kingdom belonged solely to God. The coming kingdom was essentially the coming of God in person to reveal ruling might upon the earth. The messianic hope was subordinate to the theocratic hope. The expected human or super-human deliverer was important not in himself as such, but only because he would be *Yahweh's* instrument for establishing God's kingdom or ruling in it as God's representative. (Here I am taking for granted that kingdom-expectation and messianic-hope are interrelated themes in Old Testament-Jewish eschatology. Some scholars regard them as unrelated, even alien, conceptions.[1] But as Beasley-Murray suggests, the Messiah was probably conceived as the one in whom 'God's presence is signified and the rule of the world actualised. In the person of Messiah God's purpose in history finds its embodiment.')[2]

Jesus' conception of the kingdom was also thoroughly theocentric, and he spoke only obliquely of his own messianic status. Nevertheless the Gospel tradition is quite unambiguous that as far as Jesus was concerned, the future dominion of God was uniquely concentrated in his own person,

---

1   For example, S. Mowinckel, *He That Cometh* (Oxford: OUP, 1954)
2   Beasley-Murray, *Kingdom of God*, 25

words and deeds.[1] Jesus considered himself to be, as Son of Man, the divine agent who embodied the promised sovereignty of God.[2] In his activity could be seen the action of God to set up God's rule.

We mentioned at the outset of this study that one of the differences between the pre-Easter preaching of Jesus to the post-Easter preaching of the first Christians is that the Proclaimer became the Proclaimed. The person who had announced God's kingdom became himself the object of Christian proclamation. But this difference is not as radical as it might appear. For in his role as *the* Proclaimer of the kingdom, Jesus had already laid claim to a unique role in the realisation of that kingdom. 'The Jesus of history cannot be compared to the announcer in the airline terminal who signals the arrival of plane. There is much more involvement between Jesus and his message than that simplistic analogy suggests'.[3] Rather, even when he functions as the Proclaimer of God's kingdom, Jesus is himself simultaneously the one who is proclaimed.[4]

Hence in the Gospels, to respond favourably to Jesus is to 'receive' the kingdom; to reject him is not merely to forego the immediate blessings of the kingdom's presence but also to exclude oneself from its future consummation.[5] For the link between the present and future dimensions of God's kingdom lies in Jesus' own person. As the one appointed by God

---

1 'Jesus saw the kingdom of God to be present before the parousia, which he thought to be imminent, only in his person and works; he knows no other realisation of the eschatological consummation', Kümmel, *Promise and Fulfilment*, 140, cf. 155

2 Cf. Dan 7:13ff

3 Charlesworth, *Jesus within Judaism*, 155

4 Cf. W. Marxsen, *The Beginnings of Christology* (Philadelphia: Fortress Press, 1970) 80-81

5 For example, Mark 8:35-38/Matt 16:24-28/Luke 9:23-27; Mark 10:23-31/Matt 19:23-30/Luke 18:24-30; Matt 25:31-46

to bring in God's universal cosmic dominion,[1] he had appeared on earth prior to fulfilling this future task in order to confer on people the blessings of the coming age in advance of its full realisation. How one responded to his appearance now determined how one would stand at his future coming.

No single formula can do justice to Jesus' role in the operation of the kingdom. Beasley-Murray proposes a variety of epithets for the way Jesus pictured his own task. He is the *Champion or Contender* for the *kingdom*,[2] the *Initiator*,[3] *Instrument*,[4] *Representative*,[5] *Revealer,*[6] *Mediator,*[7] and *Bearer* [8] of the kingdom.[9] The only umbrella term that can comprehend these many tasks is that of 'Messiah'.

Now it is not simply that Jesus presented himself as the decisive agent in God's kingdom that sets him apart from contemporary Jewish expectation. Some such a role was anticipated for the Messiah. Rather it was the *kind* of messianic agent he represented. He came not as an all-conquering Davidic hero, but as a lowly, suffering servant who wanted 'not to be served but to serve and to give his life a ransom for many.'[10] He came initially not as a cosmic Son of Man on the clouds of heaven, but as an earthly Son of Man who allowed himself to be betrayed, mocked, scourged, and crucified.[11] For many people, a Messiah who merely saved

---

1   Mark 13:24-27/Matt 24:29-31/Luke 21:25-28; Luke 17:20-37; 19:11ff; Mark
     14:62/Matt 24:30
2   Mark 3:27; cf. Luke 10:8
3   Matt 11:12
4   Matt 12:28
5   Luke 17:20f
6   Mark 4:11f; Matt 11:25f
7   Mark 2:18f
8   Matt 11:5
9   Beasley-Murray, *Kingdom of God*, 269
10   Mark 10:45
11   Mark 8:31; 9:3, 11; 10:32

others from demons and disease but did nothing to save himself or his nation from Rome was not worthy of belief.[1]

Yet Jesus dared to suggest that it was only through his vicarious death on a criminal's cross that the toe-hold or bridgehead of the kingdom could be established, the way cleared for the final great revelation of Yahweh's saving majesty. The Last Supper traditions make it clear that Jesus viewed his death as integral to the coming of the kingdom.[2] Some of the sayings that underline the temporal imminence of the kingdom may in fact relate to his impending passion rather than his parousia.[3] For, as Yoder puts it, 'the cross is not a detour or hurdle on the way to the kingdom, nor is it even the way to the kingdom; it is the kingdom come.'[4]

Summary

We have considered in this chapter some of the distinctive contours of Jesus' conception of the kingdom of God. Like his compatriots, Jesus conceived of the kingdom as God's dynamic, powerful rule. Like them he looked to the future for the ultimate and definitive manifestation of God's

---

1   Mark 15:29-32/Matt 27:39-44/Luke 23:35-37
2   Mark 14:22-31; Matt 26:26-30; Luke 22:15-20; cf. 1 Cor 11:23-25. Critics of contemporary 'kingdom theology' often object that it leaves no room for the proclamation of the Cross. But for Jesus, the Cross was integral to the work and character of the kingdom. See R.H. Fuller, *The Mission and Achievement of Jesus* (London: SCM, 1974), 50-78
3   See C.C. Caragounis, 'Kingdom of God, Son of Man and Jesus' Self-Understanding', Part 1 in *Tyndale Bulletin* 40 (1989), 3-23; Part 2 in *Tyndale Bulletin* 40.2 (1989), 223-238 (see esp. 233ff)
4   J.H. Yoder, *The Politics of Jesus* (Grand Rapids: Eerdmans, 1972), 61

cosmic lordship, the judgment of God's enemies and the setting up of a realm of peace and justice. He used stock Jewish images (weddings, feasts, harvests, and so on) and traditional apocalyptic motifs to picture this state of affairs. In common with mainstream Judaism, he stressed the role of repentance in preparation for God's self-disclosure[1] and understood the coming of the kingdom to be the ultimate fulfilment of Israel's destiny.

But he went beyond any of his contemporaries by boldly declaring that God's saving reign was already making itself felt in his own person and works. People did not have to wait until the future age to begin to experience the benefits of the coming triumph of God. For the one destined to bring in the new age had appeared on earth, as a kind of advance party of the approaching kingdom, to overthrow the spiritual powers arrayed against God's dominion and to mediate to those with receptive faith something of the spiritual and physical wholeness that belongs to God's new order. This was the 'gospel of the kingdom,' the good news of the presence of salvation.

---

1   That Jesus demanded repentance in response to his message has been strongly
     contested recently by E.P. Sanders, *Jesus and Judaism*, 106-113. But see B.D.
     Chilton, 'Jesus and the Repentance of E.P. Sanders', *Tyndale Bulletin* 39 (1988),
     1-18. The crucialness, in Jesus' teaching, of a human ethical response to the
     divine initiative is helpfully discussed in B.D. Chilton and J.I.H. MacDonald,
     Jesus and the Ethics of the Kingdom (London: SPCK, 1987)

4

The Operation of God's Kingdom

W e said at the outset that our aim was not to provide a single definition of the kingdom of God in the teaching of Jesus. Already we have seen that his conception is too diverse and many-sided to be easily reduced to a simple formula. It evokes a network of ideas, associations and metaphors. Nonetheless I do believe it is possible to identify three major facets of Jesus' kingdom proclamation that will not only go a long way towards providing a kind of summary-definition of what he meant by the phrase, but also offers the Church a broad agenda for preaching and extending God's kingdom today. Space only permits an outline treatment of each area, and the difficult hermeneutical issues involved in making the transposition from the first-century world of Jesus to the twentieth-century world of the contemporary Church cannot be addressed here. We must remain at the level of broad generalisation. It seems to me, however, that the good news of the advent of God's kingdom meant three main things to Jesus, three things that continue to challenge those who would follow Jesus today.

Eschatological Power

First of all, it meant *the presence of God's end-time power to put things right on the earth.* The ancient Jewish hope for the coming of the kingdom was for the coming of God 'in strength'[1] to set right what was wrong on the earth and to bring to pass a transfiguration of creation to reflect perfectly God's own good purposes. In Jesus, 'the Mightier One,' the very

---

1   Isa 40:10 LXX; cf. Mark 1:7

power that would accomplish this future transformation was operative to bring the deliverance promised for the future into the present.

Jesus was possessed of a 'salvation-energy' that had a double effect in his ministry. On the cosmic level, it brought about the plundering of Satan's *basileia* by the power of the eschatological Spirit.[1] On the human level, it involved the liberation of men and women from the effects of sin, sickness and demonic control. In Luke's narrative, at the beginning of his ministry Jesus is anointed with the Spirit of power to equip him to 'preach good news to the poor, to proclaim release to the captives, the recovery of sight to the blind, to let the oppressed go free, to proclaim the year of the Lord's favour.'[2] This *word* of release was accompanied by *acts* of release which served as concrete demonstrations of the advancing kingdom. The *dunameis* ('miracles') served as parabolic signs of the God's eschatological *dunamis* ('power') at work in the world.[3]

All the miracles predicted in Isaiah as accompanying the advent of God's reign are evidenced in the ministry of Jesus — the blind see again, the deaf hear and the lame walk, even the dead are raised.[4] The feeding miracles typify eschatological provision for the hungry. The calming of storms points to the reassertion of divine sovereignty over rebellious nature. Many sayings make this function of miracles as signs of the kingdom clear, but two are particularly striking.

---

1   Matt 12:28/Luke 11:20
2   Cf. Luke 3:22; 4:1, 14, 18
3   Cf. Mark 5:30; 6:2, 5, 44 and Mark 9:1; 13:26; 14:62. I have discussed this in relation to Mark's Gospel in my book *Faith as a Theme in Mark's Narrative* (Cambridge: CUP, 1989), 57-74
4   Cf. Isa 29:17-19; 35:5f; 42:6f with Matt 8:16f; 11:2-6; 15:30f; Mark 7:37; Luke 4:18-21

But if it is by the Spirit of God/finger of God that I cast out demons, then the kingdom of God has come to you.[1]

When John heard in prison what the Messiah was doing, he sent word by his disciples and said to him, 'Are you he who is to come or are we to wait for another?' And Jesus answered them, 'Go and tell John what you hear and see: the blind receive their sight, the lame walk, the lepers are cleansed, the deaf hear, the dead are raised, and the poor have good news brought to them. And blessed is anyone who takes no offence at me.'[2]

The close link between the presence of the kingdom and the activity of the Spirit suggested in the first of these sayings is significant.[3] For it was through the bestowal of the eschatological Spirit on the post-Easter community that the present realisation of kingdom-power continued to operate in the Church. 'Where Jesus spoke of the presence of the reign of God,' explains Lohfink, 'the early Church spoke of the presence of the Spirit. The language thus changed as a result of the experience after Easter. But the basic line of Jesus' message was continued. The future of eschatological salvation had already begun.'[4]

In anticipation of this, during his earthly ministry Jesus delegated his own eschatological authority to his disciples as an integral part of their kingdom preaching task .

---

1   Matt 12:28/Luke 11:20
2   Matt 11:2-6/Luke 7:22-23
3   Cf. also Luke 4:14, 18ff; 10:21; Acts 10:38. This relationship has been explored extensively by J.D.G. Dunn in his many writings on the Spirit in the New Testament. See especially his *Jesus and the Spirit* (London: SCM, 1975), 41-94
4   G. Lohfink, *Jesus and Community* (London: SPCK, 1985), 86, cf. 88

> He went up the mountain and called to him those whom he wanted, and they came to him. And he appointed twelve, whom he also named apostles, to be with him, and to be sent out to proclaim the message and to have authority to cast out demons.[1]

> Then Jesus called the twelve together and gave them power and authority over all demons and to cure diseases, and he sent them out to proclaim the kingdom of God and to heal.[2]

> Whenever you enter a town and its people welcome you, eat what is set before you; cure the sick who are there and say to them, 'The kingdom of God has come near to you'.[3]

The miracles then were *signs of the kingdom in action*. This is not to say that they were merely *signposts* pointing away towards some abstract theological truth. They were in themselves the very actualisation of God's rule. As signs they were full of the reality they signified; they were charged with the power they represented. They were the concrete outworking of the power of the new age that had entered the world to begin to set things right in accordance with God's plan for the fullness of time.

This did not lead to a triumphalism however. Even in Jesus' ministry, the operation of divine power stood under the eschatological proviso of 'already...not yet'. He healed many sick individuals, but he did not end forever sickness and disease. He raised a few dead people, but death still

---

1   Mark 3:13-15/Matt 10:1-4
2   Luke 9:1-2
3   Luke 10:8-9

held its sway. He fed hungry multitudes, but famine and injustice continued. He set at liberty those oppressed by the devil, but the Roman oppressors remained. He brought *shalom*, but suffered violence. He delivered others from danger, but was himself put to death. The kingdom had begun its operation, but only the future consummation would see the full renovation of the cosmos. And the miracles were intended as confirmation of this promise and as provisional signs that the process had now been set in motion. Rottenberg expresses this well.

> When Jesus healed a person, this was a sign of *shalom*, a foretaste of the time when humanity and world shall be whole. When Jesus fed people, that too was a sign of the new tomorrow, a present manifestation of the promise that humanity shall not always live in a world where some people starve in the midst of abundance. When a person found forgiveness in the presence of Jesus, it was a sign of the day when all captivity shall be made captive by the power of God. And when a person who had gained his wealth in ways that are not in accordance with the laws of the kingdom decided to pay compensation to those whom he had wronged, that was sign of the new order of things in which justice and righteousness shall prevail.[1]

It should be noted furthermore that the power of the kingdom was available not purely for therapeutic purposes. It is striking that in Mark's Gospel we find an almost identical reference to God's omnipotence (*panta dunata*, 'all things are possible') in three quite diverse settings: as power

---

1   I.C. Rottenberg, *The Promise and the Presence* (Grand Rapids: Eerdmans, 1980),
     58

to heal and drive out demons, as power to free the wealthy from devotion to their wealth, and as power to face otherwise unbearable suffering.[1]

As the community of those who have 'tasted of the powers of the age to come',[2] surely the Church's proclamation of the kingdom today should be attended by the demonstration of God's power to put things right. 'For the kingdom of God depends not on talk but on power'.[3] The charismatic renewal has reminded the Church of that salient fact.[4] As long as we recognise that the operation of divine power stands under the 'already...not yet' tension; that our experience of healing power will always be only partial until the consummation, for only then will God wipe away every tear from our eyes and death, mourning, crying and pain will be no more;[5] and that the availability of kingdom power relates as much to freedom from materialism and to strength to suffer as to miraculous healing — then we shall remain true to the perspective of Jesus.

The Nearness of God

The second thing Jesus meant by the advent of God's reign was *the closeness of God's personal presence to bring men and women into new relationship with God.*

---

1   Cf. Mark 9:23; 10:27 and 14:36
2   Heb 6:5
3   1 Cor 4:20; cf. 2:4f
4   For a brief and balanced assessment on the place of miracles in the New Testament and today, see D. Wenham, 'Miracles Then and Now', *Themelios* 12, 1 (1986), 1-4. See also the excellent article by Max Turner, 'Spiritual Gifts Then and Now', *Vox Evangelica* XV (1985), 7-64
5   Rev 21:4

We have noted a number of times that the heart of Old Testament-Jewish hope for the coming of the kingdom was for the coming of God to rule, personally as it were, upon the earth. Just how God would manifest God's personal presence is not clear, but 'for those circles in which the coming of the Messiah was an attested element in the expectation of the coming of the kingdom of God, the name "Immanuel" — God with us — is not a misleading representation of the Messiah.'[1] He would be the form of Yahweh's presence in the kingdom.

In Jesus the personal presence of God dwelt to an unparalleled degree. God's sovereignty manifested itself in Jesus not just as tremendous power but also as a yearning love that reached out to lost humanity to draw it into a new relationship of intimacy with God. This is beautifully expressed in the parable of the prodigal son.[2] Here Jesus depicts the sovereignty of God in terms of a parental love that delights to forgive the wayward child and celebrates the renewal of relationship with a joyous banquet. Three words capture the essence of this parable and sum up the second dimension of Jesus' kingdom preaching — forgiveness, fellowship, and fatherhood.

Forgiveness: It was generally held in Jesus' day that the last great act of eschatological salvation would be the final and definitive forgiveness of sins.[3] Thus when on occasions during his ministry Jesus explicitly forgave the sins of repentant individuals,[4] he was signalling the presence of the awaited kingdom.

---

1   G.R. Beasley-Muray, *Jesus and the Kingdom of God* (Grand Rapids: Eerdmans, 1986, 25
2   Luke 15:11-32
3   Cf. Isa 33:24; Jer 31-34; Mic 7:18-20; Zech 13:1
4   Mark 2:12/Matt 9:1-8/Luke 5:17-26; Luke 7:36-50

This was an audacious thing for Jesus to do. The pardoning of sins was strictly a divine prerogative,[1] and it was not anticipated that the Messiah or any other eschatological figure would possess the authority to remit sins. But God was so uniquely present in Jesus that he was able to mediate the forgiving love of God directly to sinners, although to scribal ears it amounted to blasphemy.[2] Then at the end of his life Jesus announced the sealing of the awaited new covenant of forgiveness. 'For this is my blood of the covenant which is poured out for many for the forgiveness of sins'.[3]

Fellowship: The metaphor of a feast or banquet was a common Jewish picture for eschatological salvation,[4] and Jesus frequently used it in his parables.[5] But Jesus went further and acted out his parables in life. His habit of having table fellowship with tax collectors and sinners, which earned him such notoriety,[6] was intended as a concrete anticipation of the eschatological feast.

These were no ordinary meals, for they openly breached religious custom. Jesus was enjoying the most intimate form of fellowship possible with 'members of professions which were regarded as especially

---

1   Ex 34:6f; Ps 103:3; Isa 43:25f; 44:22
2   Mark 2:7/Matt 9:3/Luke 5:21
3   Matt 26:28; cf. Jer 31:31-34
4   Cf. Isa 48:21; 49:9f; 55:1-2; Ezek 34:23f; Zech 9:17
5   For example, Mark 2:19f/Matt 9:15/Luke 5:34f; Matt 22:2-14/Luke 14:15-24
6   Mark 2:15-17/Matt 2:13-17/Luke 5:27-32; Matt 11:19; Luke 15:1-2; 19:1-10

susceptible to the transgression of God's Law'.[1] In this Jesus differed enormously from his contemporaries. John the Baptist withdrew into the wilderness to await the penitent; the Essenes of Qumran retreated into closed communities; Pharisees kept themselves pure from defilement with sinners; the Sadducees curried favour with the foreign ruling elite at the expense of the ordinary people; and the Zealots were prepared to murder 'defiled' Jews whom they considered to be collaborators with Rome. Jesus however, acting implicitly in the stead of God, sought out sinners and in his table communion with them summoned them to repentance by communicating to them the tangible experience of end-time acceptance. In this,

> Jesus was going beyond showing compassion and friendship to the unfortunate and the outcasts; he was bringing the redeeming grace of God into the lives of sinful men and women, providing the means by which they might become different people in a new relation to God, experiencing the renewing powers of the divine sovereignty and subjecting themselves to it.[2]

1   W.G. Kümmel, *A Theology of the New Testament* (SCM, London, 1973), 45. Against E.P. Sanders who denies that Jesus' concern for sinners would have offended other Jews, Charlesworth reaffirms that 'in first-century Palestine many — and not just some — Jews would have been offended by Jesus ' inclusion of sinners, such as prostitutes and tax-collectors, into his group. Certainly the pious Jews still living near Qumran, the Sadducees and other priests administering sacrifices in the Temple cult, the zealous ones (the forerunners of the Zealots), the strict Pharisees and even the conservative "people of the land" would have found Jesus' message and call to sinners to be offensive. Jesus attempted to shatter the boundaries that had been constructed by many Jewish groups to separate the pure from the impure and the righteous from the unrighteous', *Jesus Within Judaism* (London: SPCK, 1988) 207

2   Beasley-Murray, *Kingdom of God*, 270

Fatherhood: The good news of the kingdom was the good news of the closeness of God. And perhaps the most characteristic way Jesus communicated the nearness of God was by addressing God as 'Father'. The kingdom of God was the kingdom of a Father.[1] It was the *Father's* good pleasure to bestow the *kingdom* on the disciples.[2] The inseparability of the two concepts[3] is also apparent in the Lord's Prayer: 'Our *Father* who is in heaven, hallowed be your name, your *kingdom* come.'

Now Jesus did not invent 'Father' as an address for God.[4] It was not unknown in first-century Judaism for God to be spoken of as a Father.[5] Yet there was something distinctive, even unique, in Jesus' *awareness* of God's Fatherhood and his communication of it, even if the concept of divine fatherhood and the corresponding form of address were an established part of contemporary Judaism.[6] This distinctiveness lies in four main directions:

---

1   Matt 13:43; 25:34; 26:29; Luke 22:29
2   Luke 12:32
3   On this inseparability, see, e.g., G.E. Ladd, *A Theology of the New Testament* (Grand Rapids: Eerdmans, 1974), 84-87; A.M. Hunter, *Introducing New Testament Theology* (London: SCM, 1957), 31-33
4   The seminal work on Jesus' conception of God's Fatherhood was done by J. Jeremias, *The Central Message of the New Testament* (London: SCM, 1965), 9-30, idem, *The Prayers of Jesus* (London: SCM, 1967), 11-65. Although his conclusions have been qualified by subsequent research (see below), it is still the case Jeremias highlighted a crucial characteristic of Jesus' language.
5   See Deut 32:6; 2 Sam 7:14; 1 Chr 17:13; 22:10; 28:6; Pss 68:5; 89:26; 103:13; Isa 63:16; 64:8; Jer 3:4; 19; 31:9; Mal 1:6; 2:10; Job 13:4; Eccl 23:1, 5, 10; Wis Sol 2:16; 14:3; Jub 1:24-25, 28; J Lev 18:6; T. Judah 24:2; 1 Qs 9:35; B. Tann 25b; Eighteen Benedictions, Petitions 5 & 6
6   Jeremias almost certainly overstated his case by claiming that Jesus was totally unique in addressing God as Abba and in the significance he saw in the term itself. For two recent and important evaluations of the evidence, see William A. Van Gemeren, '*ABBA* in the Old Testament', *Journal of the Evangelical Theological Society* 31, 4 (1988), 385-98, and J. Barr; '"Abba Father" and the Familiarity of Jesus' Speech', *Theology* 91 (1988), 173-79; idem, 'Abba isn't "Daddy"', *Journal of Theological Studies* 39 (1988), 28-47

(i) The first is the sheer *frequency and consistency* of his use of 'Father' for God. Certainly there are several references to the Fatherhood of God in the wealth of Jewish literature. But whereas the rabbis would occasionally refer to God's Fatherhood, Jesus placed excessive emphasis on it.

(ii) Jesus was distinctive in freely using the *personal pronoun* 'my' in speaking of God as Father,[1] thereby laying claim to a unique filial relationship to God. Although the evidence is disputed,[2] it seems that individual Jews of Jesus' time were scarcely in the habit of calling God 'my Father' as easily and naturally as Jesus did.

(iii) Significantly, Jesus chose to use the *everyday Aramaic expression 'Abba'* for God rather than the more formal terminology of liturgical Hebrew. 'Abba' was a term used within the family circle, and as such expressed familiarity and security. Even if 'Abba' did not necessarily have the childish ring of 'daddy', as popularly thought,[3] it remains true that Jesus spoke to God as easily and intimately as one would speak to one's natural father.[4] It is not clear whether Jesus only or always used 'Abba' for God. But the fact that early Greek-speaking Christians adopted the

---

1   Matt 11:27
2   Cf. J.D.G. Dunn, *Jesus and the Spirit*, 23. See the balanced treatment by D.A. Hagner *The Jewish Reclamation of Jesus* (Grand Rapids: Zondervan, 1984) 209-211
3   See J. Barr, "'Abba Father", 175ff
4   Charlesworth thinks it conceivable that Jesus chose the Aramaic 'Abba' rather than the Hebrew term *'abinu*, 'because he had a conception of God that was in some ways different from that of *most* of his contemporaries. Many early Jews *tended* to conceive of God as distant, visiting humanity only through intermediaries such as angels, as we know from studying the Pseudepigrapha and the Dead Sea Scrolls. Jesus perceived that God himself was very near, and that he was directly concerned about each person, even (perhaps especially) sinners', *Jesus Within Judaism*, 134

practice of using this Aramaic term in prayer suggests there was something very special about Jesus' use of 'Abba' for God. [1]

(iv) Finally, Jesus linked *other peoples' experience of God's Fatherhood to their relationship with himself.* Jesus never spoke of God as the Father of Israel, much less of all humanity. The full experience of this relationship was extended only to those who responded to the message of the kingdom. Jesus applied the category of sonship only to his own followers.[2] In other words, Jesus seems to have seen a link between his disciples' sonship of God and their discipleship to him. 'Their "Abba" was somehow derived from his "Abba", their sonship from his.'[3]

Yet interestingly Jesus also maintained a distinction between his own filial relationship to God and that of his disciples. He spoke of 'my Father' and to his disciples of 'your Father',[4] but he never spoke of 'our Father' (the 'our Father' of the Lord's Prayer is a model for the *disciples* to use). John 20:17 captures this distinction well. Jesus tells Mary to 'go to my brothers and say to them, "I am ascending to my Father and to your Father, to my God and to your God"'. So distinctive was the disciples' experience of the presence of the kingdom as the closeness of God's Fatherhood that Jesus instructed them to reserve the status of 'Father' for God alone. 'Call no man on earth your father; for you have one Father who is in heaven'.[5]

---

1   Rom 8:15; Gal 4:6
2   Mark 11:25/Matt 6:15; Matt 5:48; 6:32/Luke 12:30; Matt 7:11/Luke 11:13; Luke 12:32
3   J.D.G. Dunn *Unity and Diversity in the New Testament* (London: SCM, 1977), 212. idem, *Jesus and the Spirit,* 25
4   Cf. Matt 11:27 and Matt 6:14f
5   Matt 23:9

The kingdom that has drawn near in Jesus then is the kingdom of a forgiving Father who seeks intimate fellowship with his wayward children. The Church's proclamation of the kingdom should also be characterised by this personal warmth and love. The kingdom is not just some cold blueprint for the renewal of society. It is the parental-heart of God yearning for intimacy with the creatures who bear God's image. It seems to me that this dimension of the kingdom encompasses such concerns as personal evangelism, the creative development of corporate worship, and the deepening of individual spirituality. Some activists see these areas as a pietistic diversion from the social implications of the Christian gospel. They are far from that. They are in fact integral to the conception of God's kingdom that emerges from the teaching of Jesus.

A Transformed Community

The third dimension in Jesus' programme for the establishment of God's kingdom *was the creation of a messianic community to live in a manner consistent with the demands of the new age in the midst of the old.*

We noted earlier that the reign of God necessarily creates a realm in which God's rule is experienced and enjoyed. The kingdom of God is not solely God's ruling activity; it is also the social reality created by that activity. Thus in Mark's Gospel, the first thing Jesus does after the initial kingdom announcement is to convene a discipleship community in which the rule of God might be concretely and visibly realised.[1] It is the existence of this community as a society shaped by the ethos of God's coming new order that gives the kingdom message of Jesus a definite *social and political thrust.*

It is often said that Jesus had little interest in changing the social structures of his time. 'That there is little explicit social teaching in the Gospels', says H.H. Rowden, 'indicate[s] that Jesus was more concerned with the fundamental matter of personal ethics than with the construction of a blueprint or even the enunciation of principles designed to lead to the transformation of society'.[2] Similarly I.H. Marshall insists that 'there is no programme for social action in the teaching of Jesus about the kingdom of God. He is concerned with the relationship of individuals to God and the behaviour that will result from that.'[3]

But, in my view, this way of characterising the scope of Jesus' ethical teaching is unjustifiably restrictive, and has potentially damaging

---

1   Mark 1:14-20. It is often asserted that Jesus never intended to found the Church. But, as Charlesworth notes, 'the Church ultimately derives from Jesus' conviction and proclamation that in his time and place God was calling into being a special group of people. This group constituted the small band of the faithful ones who prepared for and eargerly awaited God's final act before the end of all normal history and time. Jesus apparently never envisioned or found a "Church" of Jews and Gentiles. Yet, his calling into being an eschatological community under God's reign provided the inspiration and the impetus from which the Church eventually shaped itself', *Jesus within Judaism*, 17

2   H.H. Rowden, 'Ethics', in M.C. Tenney (ed.), *Zondervan Pictorial Encyclopedia of the Bible* (Grand Rapids: Zondervan, 1975), 410. O. Barclay maintains that the 'kingdom theme has biblically much to say about personal ethics and the Church but, I submit, virtually nothing to say about social ethics in a mixed society,' 'The Theology of Social Ethics: A Survey of Current Positions', *Interchange* 36 (1985), 9

3   I.H. Marshall, 'The Hope of a New Age: The Kingdom of God in the New Testament', *Themelios* 11, 1 (1985), 9. To be fair, Marshall does go on to stress that the proclamation of the kingdom has social and communal implications.

implications for Christian witness. Certainly it is true that Jesus did not speculate about the nature of human society in the manner of a Greek philosopher. He was a prophet not a philosopher. Nor did he lay out a master-plan for the operation of societal structures. Had he done so, it would long since have become obsolete and irrelevant. But this does not mean that there is no social dimension to Jesus' ethical teaching, or that he was concerned only with moral and spiritual matters and kept himself aloof from the political, military and social issues of his day.

When it is remembered that the people of Jesus' day lacked the excessive individualism of modern Western society and derived their sense of identity and worth from their solidarity with the wider community, the idea that Jesus could speak to the needs of individuals without *at the same time* addressing the life of the whole community, is inconceivable. Furthermore, the modern distinction between religious and political life would be quite alien to ancient Jewish society. The religious leaders of Jesus' day also exercised political power; the law of Moses was the law of the land; the Temple was the centre of spiritual and civil authority, as well as the powerhouse of the Jerusalem economy; the Sanhedrin was the major arm of domestic government; and the Jerusalem authorities were finally responsible to the Roman governor.

In view of this, Jesus' message and lifestyle, his disregard for certain traditions and customs, his reinterpretation of the Law, his claim to royal (messianic) authority, his high-handed action in the Temple precincts, and much more, would have been perceived as a challenge to the very cornerstones of Jewish society and ultimately to the Roman provincial peace. It is not surprising therefore that in the Gospels those who are most antagonistic to Jesus' proclamation of the rule of God are those in positions of religious, political and military power in the ruling establishment of

Israel, both Jewish and Gentile. They had a vested interest in the way things were and had most to lose from Jesus' demand for the reordering of personal and social relationships in accordance with the eschatological will of God.[1]

In short, Jesus' message of the dawning kingdom had very definite social and political implications.[2] It is a drastic impoverishment of his message and a blunting of its radical edge to suggest that Jesus was concerned only with the spiritual needs and personal conduct of isolated individuals. The key thing to recognise is the *methodology* Jesus proposed to initiate social renewal.

I would suggest that Jesus' proclamation of the kingdom of God included an implicit strategy for social renewal which entailed a prophetic denunciation of the injustices and hypocrisy of surrounding society on the one hand, and the calling together of an alternative society to live according to the standards of the coming kingdom on the other. Commentators often overlook or underestimate the potential societal impact that such a 'contrast society', planted in the heart of mainstream society, is capable of. But, as G. Lohfink observes,

---

1 See Marshall, *Faith as a Theme*, 179-82
2 See the helpful discussion by S. Mott, *Jesus and Social Ethics* (Bramcote, Notts: Grove Books, no.55, 1984)

> The anti-social and corrupt systems of a dominant society cannot be attacked more sharply than by the formation of an anti-society in its midst. Simply through its existence, this new society is a more efficacious attack on the old structures than any program, without personal cost, for the general transformation of the world.[1]

This twofold strategy is evident in at least four major areas of contemporary social life addressed by Jesus. In his teaching Jesus exhibited:

(i) A Rejection of Social Prejudice: Supremely characteristic of Jesus was his orientation to the social margins — the destitute, the weak, social outcasts, women, children, Gentiles, Samaritans, the physically deformed, the sick, the possessed. The dawning of the kingdom of God, said Jesus, was good news for the socially disadvantaged.[2] Why? Because those who are powerless in human terms are usually more open to the power or Rule of God than are the powerful. They literally have nothing to lose but their chains! It was good news also because, as every Jew knew, the coming of the kingdom meant the exertion of divine justice on behalf of the oppressed.

---

1   Lohfink *Jesus and Community*, 95. Yoder makes a similar observation: 'New teachings are no threat, as long as the teacher stands alone; a movement, extending his personality in both time and space, presenting an alternative to the structures that were there before, challenges the system as no mere words could ever do,' J.H. Yoder, *The Politics of Jesus* (Grand Rapids: Eerdmans, 1972), 40

2   Luke 4:18ff; Matt 11:2-6/Luke 7:18-35

Jesus opposed social prejudice in two ways. On the one hand, he openly criticised the smug superiority of the religious Establishment,[1] and knowingly offended them by seeking intimate fellowship with outcasts.[2] On the other hand, he assembled a new community in which the poor were to be given preference,[3] the sick and the imprisoned cared for,[4] women accorded dignity and equality,[5] children esteemed as models to be emulated,[6] and Gentiles and Samaritans embraced as full members.[7]

(ii) A Distrust of Wealth: It is surely impossible to read Luke's gospel without sensing Jesus' profound hostility to materialism.[8] As an alternative source of security, surplus wealth created a barrier to God and to the radical demands of God's kingdom.[9] As well as that, the concentration of massive riches in the hands of a few was evidence of structural injustice in society. The rich prospered at the expense of the poor. Jesus' statement, 'for you always have the poor with you',[10] should not be taken as a sign of his passive acquiescence to poverty in society. It

---

1   For example, Matt 9:13; 21:31; Luke 6:24f; 16:15
2   For example, Mark 2:15ff/Matt 9:10ff/Luke 5:27ff; Matt 11:19/Luke 15:1f; 19:1-10
3   For example, Luke 14:12ff
4   Matt 25:31-46
5   For example, Luke 8:1-3; 10:38-42; Mark 14:3-9; 15:40f; John 3:7-38
6   Mark 9:36, 42/Matt 18:1-5/Luke 9:46-48; Mark 10:13-16/Matt 19:13-15/Luke 18:15-17
7   For example, Mark 7:24-30/Matt 15:21-28; Mark 11:17; 13:10; Matt 8:5-13/Luke 7:1-10; Matt 12:18; 21:43/Luke 20:16; Matt 28;19f; Luke 9:51-55; John 4:7-42
8   Such hostility is not confined to Luke's Gospel alone. See T.E. Schmidt, *Hostility to Wealth in the Synoptic Gospels* (Sheffield: JSOT Press, 1987)
9   Mark 4:19/Matt 13:22/Luke 8:14; Mark 10:17-31/Matt 19:16-30/Luke 18:18-30; Matt 6:21, Luke 12:16-21; 14:1-14; 16:13)
10   Mark 14:7/Matt 26:11/John 12:8

is in fact an implied rebuke, for according to Deut 15:11 enduring poverty was evidence of a failure to keep the laws of the covenant.

Jesus' use of the intriguing term 'mammon of injustice' (*mamona tes adikias*)[1] may even imply that he saw in wealth an inherent tendency towards injustice. Wealth embodies a spiritual force that encourages corruption and seeks to enslave people by demanding idolatrous worship and service.[2] This is confirmed in Jesus' overt attack on the greedy rich of his day.[3] 'Woe to you who are rich, for you have received your consolation. Woe to you who are full now, for you will be hungry'.[4] Jesus criticised the rich for three related sins: for accumulating unneeded surplus;[5] for ignoring the needs of the poor;[6] and for their corruption and exploitation of the weak.[7]

By contrast, Jesus pronounced beatitude upon the poor. 'Blessed are you who are poor, for yours is the kingdom of God. Blessed are you who are hungry now, for you will be filled. Blessed are you who weep now, for you will laugh'.[8] Now Jesus is *not* here turning poverty, hunger and tears into 'spiritual values' in themselves. The poor, the starving and the

---

1   Luke 16:9
2   Luke 16:13
3   The semantic force of the terms 'rich' and 'poor' in the Gospels has been the subject of considerable discussion. Whereas we moderns understand these labels in *quantitative* economic terms, in the ancient world they were also *qualitative* categories. They designated *types* of people and the circumstances they were in, not just *how much* they possessed. Accordingly in Jesus' teaching, the 'poor' and 'rich' stand for the *needy and the greedy*. See B.J. Malina, 'Wealth and Poverty in the New Testament and its World', *Interpretation* 41 (1987), 354-67
4   Luke 6:24f
5   Luke 12:15-21; 16:19; 21:1-4; Matt 11:8
6   Luke 10:25-37; 16:19-27
7   Mark 11:15-19; Mark 12:40/Luke 20:47; Matt 23:23ff/Luke 11:42f
8   Luke 6:20f/Matt 5:3ff

sorrowful are not blessed because of their condition but because God intends to reverse their situation through bringing in his kingdom. When the future kingdom comes in its fullness, poverty and pain will be no more. In the meantime, the power of the kingdom is present to bring healing and liberation; to create a new community to work against poverty, hunger and misery. As Klaus Wengst puts it:

> Thus here we are clearly shown one aspect of what the kingdom of God means for Jesus: it is the conquest of poverty and need, the laughter of the liberated, whose oppression and grief has come to an end...Thus the beatitudes prove also to be declarations of war against poverty, hunger and tears: they are concerned for radical change. They look to the coming kingdom of God for this change; the reasons given in the second and third beatitudes are future forms. But this expectation is not just to be waited for; it has a reality in behaviour to match. When Jesus turns to those on the periphery, in his fellowship with his followers, people are already filled, already laugh, who would otherwise be pushed aside and have nothing to laugh about. So we are to see as an expression of this the way in which the reason put in the first beatitude is put in the present: the kingdom of God is now already an event in symbolic anticipation, in which the hungry are filled and those who weep laugh, in which, in the community of equals, the domination of one person by another has come to an end.[1]

---

1   Klaus Wengst, *Pax Romana and the Peace of Christ* (London: SCM, 1987), 65. Haughey comments of Luke's text: 'We do violence to the realism of Judaism if we choose to hear the terms which connote poverty, bondage, deprivation and oppression as metaphors referring to the 'spiritual life'. If they do not mean what they say, if Luke's Jesus is suggesting that the political and economic order and the world of social systems are to be circumvented in order for his hearers to be religious, then he has certainly chosen a peculiar text for saying so', John C. Haughey, S.J. 'Jesus as the Jusice of God', in John C. Haughey (ed.), *The Faith That Does Justice: Examing the Christian Sources for Social Change* (New York/Ramsey/Toronto: Paulist Press, 1977), 270

Not only are the poor and hungry to find dignity and acceptance within the new community, but a whole new attitude to material possessions is to prevail therein. Following Jesus entails a commitment to share one's material resources with those in need.[1] A lifestyle of simplicity,[2] material dependence[3] and constant vigilance against the 'lure of wealth',[4] are to be the hallmarks of the kingdom community.

(iii) A Suspicion of Worldly Power: The kingdom of God was inaugurated by Jesus in the context of an occupied country. Rome was the superpower of the day. The Jews, along with most other nations, languished under the *Pax Romana.* A key element in Roman administration was the policy of indirect rule. Ultimate power resided in Rome, but indigenous rulers were allowed to exercise jurisdiction over their own territories — as long as they did so in the interests of the Imperium. In Jesus' day, Galilee was controlled by Herod Antipas, while Judea was controlled by a Roman Governor, Pontius Pilate, though internal affairs were administered by the Jewish Sanhedrin.

As a result, Jesus was confronted by three main forms of institutional power: the spiritual and domestic authority of the Jewish religious leaders; the civil authority of Herod and the Herodians; and the imperial and military authority of Rome. And he expressed criticism of the way *all three* exercised their power.[5] The basic presupposition of his political

---

1   For example, Mark 10:17-30; Matt 6:2-4; Matt 7:7-11; Luke 6:35, 38; 8:1-3;
       12:32-34; 19:1-10; 14:25-35; John 12:6; 13:29
2   Matt 6:19-34/Luke 12:22-31
3   Mark 6:7-13, cf. Luke 9:38; 10:4
4   Mark 4:19
5   See the brief summary in M. Hengel, *Christ and Power* (Dublin: Christian
       Journals, 1977), 15-21

critique was that sovereignty or kingship (*basileia*) belongs to God. God alone possesses ultimate authority in human affairs, and *God's* character, *God's* demands, *God's* standards, are the measuring rod against which the exercise of human power is to be evaluated.

Throughout his ministry Jesus was steadfastly opposed by the *Jewish leaders*, both Pharisee and Sadducee. Clearly they felt threatened by Jesus' call for the reordering of religious and social life in light of the dawning kingdom. Jesus responded to their opposition with blistering denunciations of their conduct and role in society. The most extensive example of his attack on the scribes and Pharisees is found in Matthew 23. A careful reading of this chapter shows that it was not their theological views that Jesus objected to; it was their misuse of religious power. They used the Law to overburden the weak without lifting a finger to help. They majored on legal trivia while neglecting the weightier matters of justice, mercy and faithfulness. They appeared respectable on the outside but were full of extortion and greed within. They condemned the violence of the past, but were more than ready to shed innocent blood themselves. They claimed to be guardians of divine truth, but luxuriated in the prestige and kudos afforded their position in society. In other places in the Gospels too, the religious authorities are denounced for their greed, corruption, dishonesty, hypocrisy and violence.[1]

In Mark 3:6 and 12:15, the *Herodians* join forces with the Jewish leaders to destroy Jesus; they too were threatened by him. When some

---

1   For example, Mark 7:6-23; 12:1-12, 38-44; 13:9f; Luke 11:37-53; 16:14f; 18:9-14

sympathetic Pharisees warn Jesus that Herod Antipas is out to kill him, Jesus sends a message of defiance back to 'that fox'.[1] In so doing Jesus both likens his own native ruler to a destructive little animal and denies him any authority over his mission. The agenda of the kingdom has priority over Herod's plans. Later when tried by Herod, Jesus refuses to co-operate with his interrogation.[2]

Jesus was also critical of *Roman* power. Now it is true that Jesus never voiced direct opposition to Roman rule. He never called for the removal of the Romans from Judea, and certainly did not adopt a Zealot stance. But this does not mean that he approved of the Roman order or was indifferent to it. Several considerations show that he was far from being detached from this issue.

To begin with, Jesus' entire mission *presupposed* a repudiation of the Roman boast that Roman might had already introduced the Golden Age of 'peace and stability.' Jesus proclamation of the kingdom of God was tantamount to a rejection of the *Pax Romana* as the order intended by God. As Wengst observes, 'anyone who prays for the coming of the kingdom of God, expects it very soon, and sees the sign of its dawning in his own action, has no faith in the imperial good tidings of a pacified world and human happiness in it; he does not regard this situation as the peace that God wants, but is certain that it will end soon.'[3] Jesus regarded the Roman *Pax* as a pseudo-peace and he refused to give his blessing to it. Indeed he

---

1   Luke 13:31-33
2   Luke 23:6-12
3   Wengst, *Pax Romana*, 55

recognised that his mission would mean the destabilising of the present 'peaceful' order because it was based on oppression and injustice.[1]

As well as this, Jesus' ethical teaching and whole manner of life constituted an *implicit criticism* of the abusive power of Rome. Richard Cassidy brings this out with respect to Luke's portrait of Jesus.

> The Jesus that Luke presented to his readers is thus a figure significantly at variance with the values and the patterns in terms of which the Romans built their empire. Luke's Jesus opts for the sick and the poor; the Romans rewarded the strong. Luke's Jesus stresses humility and service; the Romans took pride in their own superiority. Luke's Jesus stresses the sharing of surplus possessions; the Romans enacted oppressive taxes in order to increase their wealth. Luke's Jesus emphasizes the sovereignty of God; the Romans affirmed pagan gods and the persona of the emperor. Luke's Jesus rejects the use of of the sword; the Romans built an empire based on violence.[2]

Consistent with this, there are also several places where Jesus *explicitly* criticises the Roman authorities for way they exercised their power. In one saying, which Luke significantly places at the Last Supper immediately prior to his arrest, Jesus underlines the coercive and self-serving nature of Roman rule.[3] In another he speaks disparagingly of the material trappings of Gentile rule and says that greater respect is owed to the least in the kingdom of God than to kings and rulers.[4] In yet another

---

1   Matt 10:34f; Luke 23:1-2; cf. John 14:27 and 18:36
2   R. J. Cassidy, *Society and Politics in the Acts of the Apostles* (Maryknoll, N.Y: Orbis Books, 1987), 17; idem, *Jesus, Politics and Society* (Maryknoll, N.Y: Orbis Books, 1983)
3   Luke 22:25/Mark 10:42/Matt 20:25
4   Matt 11:18/Luke 7:25

he anticipates violence and murderous opposition to the gospel from Gentile governors and kings.[1]

Jesus' most important statement on Roman authority occurs in the so-called 'tribute question'.[2] There is no space to give this crucial passage the careful exegesis it requires. It may be urged however that in saying 'give to the emperor the things that are the emperor's and to God the things that are God's,' Jesus was neither condoning imperial taxation *tout simple*, nor expressing indifference to the whole issue of Roman control. If his words were intended as an unambiguous affirmation of Rome's right to levy taxes, it is hard to see how his enemies could construe them as sedition.[3] Instead, side-stepping the specific issue of taxation, Jesus was pointing his questioners to a deeper underlying principle — namely that the demands of the Roman state must be critically evaluated in light of the demands of God. All things belong to God, and only insofar as the demands of Caesar are consistent with the ways of God, may they be regarded as legitimate.

As well as speaking critically of the abusive use of power in surrounding society, Jesus required his discipleship community to turn prevailing patterns of power and greatness upside down. In this new society, there is to be no hierarchy of status, as prevailed in contemporary Judaism:

---

1   Mark 13:9f/Luke 21:12f; cf. Matt 24:9
2   Mark 12:13-17/Matt 22:15-22/Luke 20:20-26
3   Luke 23:2

> But you are not to be called rabbi, for you have one teacher and you
> are all students. And call no one your father on earth, for you have
> one Father — the one in heaven. Nor are you to be called
> instructors, for you have one instructor, the Messiah. The greatest
> among you will be your servant. All who exalt themselves will be
> humbled, and all who humble themselves will be exalted.[1]

There is to be do domination of the weak by the powerful, no lording
it over one another in the manner of Gentile rulers.

> You know that among the Gentiles those whom they recognize as
> their rulers lord it over them, and their great ones are tyrants over
> them. But it is not so among you; but whoever wishes to become
> great among you must be your servant, and whoever wishes to be
> first among you must be slave of all.[2]

True greatness is shown by striving to be of least account.[3] Leadership
is servanthood.[4] And the wider social impact of the new kingdom
community is not dependent on possessing human clout and influence but
on the power of faith, prayer and forgiveness.[5]

(iv) A Repudiation of War and Violence: Jesus knew that the existing
'system' sanctioned violence to achieve its ends. He was well aware of
the brutality of Roman rule. He spoke of Pilate's ruthlessness,[6] and of how

---

1   Matt 23:8-12
2   Mark 10:42f
3   Mark 9:33-37/Matt 18:1-6/Luke 9:46-48; Mark 10:13-16/Matt 19:13-15/Luke
     18:15-17
4   Luke 22:26
5   Mark 11:20-25; on this passage, see Marshall, *Faith as a Theme*, 159-74
6   Luke 13:1

the Romans domineered their subjects.[1] He knew that he himself would
face torture and death at Roman hands,[2] and that his followers also faced
the prospect of persecution and crucifixion.[3] He spoke gravely of the time
ahead when the Romans would employ the dreadful horror of siege warfare
against Jerusalem.[4] He also knew the violence that seethed beneath the
surface of Jewish society.[5] Jesus was no starry-eyed idealist when it came
to the subject of violence!

Aware that the established order would use lethal force to oppose his
kingdom-initiative, three existing options were available to him. He could
take the Zealot option and strive to bring in the kingdom by military force.
Or he could take the Qumran option and advocate the complete withdrawal
of his messianic community from the corruption of surrounding society.
Or he could take the Establishment option and seek to make the best of a
poor situation by co-operation or collaboration. Jesus rejected all three.
Instead he chose the way of *non-violent, sacrificial love* and required the
same of his followers.[6] Jesus totally rejected war and violence as having
any place in God's kingdom. We have already discussed on this in an
earlier section and so will not elaborate on it any further here.

To sum up: the approaching kingdom impinged directly on the major
dimensions of social life — the use of wealth and power, the exclusion of
the weak and disadvantaged from full participation in the wider
community, and the use of lethal violence to protect the unjust status quo.

1   Luke 22:24-27
2   Mark 10:33-34/Matt 20:17-19/Luke 18:31-34
3   Mark 8:34-38; 13:9f/Luke 21:12f
4   Luke 19:41-44; 21:20-24; 23:27-31
5   Matt 23:29-36; Luke 9:7-9; 13:31-35; Mark 13:9ff
6   Matt 5:38-48

Jesus was critical of the prevailing social order and called for communal repentance.[1] He also laid down a new ethic for his disciples. In the eschatological community, the weak are to be honoured; wealth is to be redistributed; leadership is to take the form of servanthood; and the way of non-violent, sacrificial love is to prevail. The vision of the coming kingdom *and its righteousness or justice* is to be the supreme concern of its existence.[2] That is to say, the primary formative power over its way of life is not the past or the present but the future, the new day coming. As a colony of the age to come planted in the midst of the old order, the kingdom community is to serve *both* as an alternative expression of human society that summons mainstream society to change (a city set on a hill),[3] *and* as a subversive force for change within the existing order (salt and light).[4]

Clearly then, as Richard Horsley recognises, 'Jesus, while announcing that God was taking the initiative (the kingdom of God was at hand), emphasises that the kingdom was a matter of people renewing their *social relations* in accordance with the will and in response to the enabling presence of God.'[5] The kingdom was present not only as power and love, but also as justice and peace.

Such also is to be the concern of the Church today, even if the social matrix of the Christian community today is very different to that of

---

1   Cf. Matt 11:20-24
2   Matt 6:33
3   Matt 5:14
4   Matt 5:13, 16
5   R.A. Horsley, 'Popular Prophetic Movements at the Time of Jesus: Their Principal Features and Social Origins', *Journal for the Study of the New Testament* 26 (1986), 22 (emphasis mine)

first-century Palestine. Inasmuch as the biblical vision for the kingdom of God is the setting up of a universal realm of peace and justice on earth, the Church as an eschatological community is called to a twofold task. On the one hand, it is to proclaim the breakthrough of the future age by giving visible expression in its own life to the peace, justice and righteousness of God's kingdom. On the other hand, it is to work tirelessly for peace and justice in surrounding society, to struggle against the forces of the old age — forces of nationalism, militarism, materialism, sexism and racism — which Christ has dethroned and which one day shall finally yield to God's glorious future. 'None of our achievements, programs and projects, or our social actions, campaigns and crusades, should be absolutised as if they constituted the kingdom itself', warns Rottenberg. 'Yet, by the grace of God, the fruits of our labours, ministries and mission can become part of God's redemptive work'.[1]

Summary

We have suggested in this chapter that Jesus' proclamation of the kingdom entailed three main assertions: the presence of eschatological power to put things right upon the earth in accordance with God's ultimate intentions for the world; the closeness of God's personal presence to bring people into a new relationship with himself as a loving Father; and the creation of an alternative society to express and to work for peace and justice on earth.

---

1   Rottenberg, *Promise and Presence*, 61

If this is a fair summary of Jesus' conception of the kingdom of God, then the Church's agenda is clear, at least in broad outline. It is to heal the sick, to restore the lost to relationship with God, to incarnate an alternative way of life under the lordship of Christ, and to pray for and work towards the transformation of human society in the name of the coming reign of God. All this is implied in bearing witness to the gospel of the kingdom.

> And this good news of the kingdom will be proclaimed throughout the world, as a testimony to all nations; and then the end will come.[1]

> The kingdom of the world has become the kingdom of our Lord and of his Messiah, and he will reign forever and ever.[2]

Come the day.

---

1   Matt 24:14
2   Rev 11:15

5

A Meditation — The Precious and Costly Kingdom

S tory telling is one of the most effective methods of communication we have — something Jesus knew well, and something that makes me often lament my own ineffectiveness as a story-teller. I'm a hopeless story-teller, and can never remember any of the good stories I've heard. But, like everybody else, I love listening to stories.

Recently I read my four-year-old son a simplified version of the children's classic tale *Treasure Island*. It is the story of how the hero, Jim Hawkins, and his friends come into possession of a map showing the location of the buried treasure of the fearsome pirate Captain Flint, and go to enormous lengths and through many adventures to find it. My little boy was enthralled. He even slept with the book under his blankets that night so he could look at it again first thing in the morning.

Not only did the excitement and adventure of the story captivate him (especially the fights with the wicked pirates), but there was also something about the idea of *risking all to find hidden treasure* that even as a child he could readily identify with. Everybody can. The enormous popularity of game shows on TV is at least partly because they tap into the human desire to acquire, in one fell swoop, a vast treasure that would otherwise take years, even a lifetime, to earn.

Perhaps this is why Jesus also told stories about finding buried treasure. In two well-known little parables in Matthew 13:44-46, Jesus likens the experience of the kingdom of God to discovering hidden fortunes:

> The kingdom of heaven is like treasure hidden in a field, which someone found and hid; then in his joy he goes and sells all that he has and buys that field.

Again, the kingdom of heaven is like a merchant in search of fine pearls; on finding one pearl of great value, he went and sold all that he had and bought it.

In these twin stories,[1] Jesus uses familiar situations of everyday life to point people to a deeper truth about God's kingdom. That's what a parable always does. The first parable concerns a man who stumbles across a treasure-trove in a field he is ploughing. The man is probably an agricultural day-labourer[2], a poor man[3] hired by a large land owner on a day-by-day basis to work his property. Because of the frequency of invasions in Palestine, people often buried their treasure in the ground for

---

1   Variants of both stories recur in the Gospel of Thomas. The parable of the hidden treasure is found in logion 109, 'with a world-denying interpretation', and the parable of the pearl in logion 76, 'with a spiritual interpretation' [so J. Drury, The Parables in the Gospels (London: SPCK, 1985), 88]. J.Jeremias speaks of the 'completely distorted version of the parable of the Treasure in the Field in the Gospel of Thomas' (198), but sees Thomas' parable of the pearl as containing many of the original elements of the dominical story (199f), The Parables of Jesus (London: SCM, 1972).
     Jesus said: The kingdom of the father is like a merchant who had merchandise [and] who found a pearl. This merchant was prudent. He got rid of [i.e., sold] the merchandise and bought the one pearl for himself. You must also seek for the treasure which does not perish, which abides where no moth comes near to eat and [where] no worm destroys [*76]
     Jesus said: The kingdom is like a man who had a treasure [hidden] in his field, without knowing it. And [after] he died, he left it to his [son. The] son knew nothing [about it]. He accepted the field [and] sold [it]. And he who bought it came, [and] while he was ploughing [he found] the treasure. He began to lend money at interest to [whomever] he wished [*109]

2   On the various possibilities for the relationship between the owner and the finder, see J.D.M. Derrett, Law in the New Testament (London: Darton, Longman & Todd, 1970), 9-13. It would appear that only a day-labourer, who found a treasure by chance rather than as part of his contracted task, could legally secure that treasure by purchasing the field. If the find were made by a servant or tenant of the owner, it automatically would have belonged to the owner.

3   The poverty of the man is apparent in the fact that he has to sell up everything he possesses in order to buy a single field. So R.H. Gundry, Matthew. A Commentary on His Literary and Theological Art (Grand Rapids: Eerdmans, 1982), 278

safe-keeping. In this case, the treasure could have lain in the ground for centuries. Certainly the owner of the property knows nothing about it (or he would not have sold the field!), and according to Jewish law, he had no legal claim to it until it was lifted out of the ground; only once it was on the surface the ground would the treasure trove become his. The day-labourer was thus quite within his legal rights to leave the treasure in the ground undisturbed and to cover it over again, until he had purchased the field himself. Then, once lifted, the treasure became his.[1]

The hero of the second story is a big-businessman, a wholesale dealer[2] who would travel far and wide in search of fine pearls to buy off the pearl-fishermen who operated in the Red Sea, the Persian Gulf and the Indian Ocean.[3] Pearls fetched fantastic prices in antiquity. Cleopatra is said to have had a pearl worth 100 million sesterces (approximately $NZ 50 million).[4] Pearls then were highly prized. On one of his business trips, the merchant comes across an exquisite and flawless pearl that he simply *has* to have. So magnificent, so priceless, is this one pearl, he is prepared to sell up his entire merchandise in order to buy it.

---

1   See the discussion of the legal issues involved in Derrett, *Law in the New Testament*, 3-13. Derrett notes that most commentators either ignore the moral dilemma created by the story as it stands (viz., that Jesus appears to commend someone who takes advantage of the owner's ignorance of the treasure in the field and cheats him out of what is rightfully his), or else propose that the unscrupulous nature of the man's action is beside the point of the parable — which is simply to portray the joyful abandonment one has upon discovery of the secret of the kingdom. Derrett shows however that the man's action is to forestall the owner of the field falsely claiming that the treasure belonged to him, when in fact he had not legal rights to it at all.

2   *emporeo* marks the merchant as a wholesale dealer, a big businessman who travelled to such places [as the Red Sea, Persian Gulf and Indian Ocean], not a small-time, shopkeeping retailer *(kapelos),*' Gundry, Matthew, 279

3   See F. Hauck, *Theological Dictionary of the New Testament* IV. 472-73; Jeremias, *Parables*, 200

4   Jeremias, *Parables*, 199

Now both these parables illustrate the same point — that when a person finds something of surpassing value, he or she will spare no effort and consider no sacrifice too great, to attain it.[1] Jesus' intention is to convince his hearers that God's kingdom is like this — it is the most *precious* thing conceivable — and as such it demands the most *costly* response from those who encounter it. The parables actually call upon their hearers to do two things — firstly, *to make a discovery*, to discover the remarkable nature and priceless value of God's kingdom; and secondly, *to make a response*, a radical and costly response to that priceless reality. Let's think for a moment about each of these aspects.

A Remarkable Discovery

Both stories turn upon the idea of *discovery*, of finding something of great value that is hidden from normal sight. The repetition of the verb 'to find' in both stories draws attention to this idea of discovery.[2] In the parable of the buried treasure, the labourer stumbles across the treasure quite by chance. He's not looking for treasure, but in the course of his ploughing, finds (*hurōn*) it. In the second parable, the merchant *is* actively searching (*zētounti*) for beautiful pearls, and in the process happens upon (*hurōn*) the finest pearl he has ever seen.

---

1   T.W. Manson, *The Sayings of Jesus* (London: SCM, 1957), 196f
2   J.D. Crossan notes that the three verbs 'find-sell-buy' underline the structural sequence of both stories, *In Parables. The Challenge of the Historical Jesus* (San Francisco: Harper & Row, 1973), 34

The kingdom of God is like this, Jesus says. For some people, discovery of the kingdom will be an unexpected joy, pure serendipity, something they're not even looking for but come across almost by accident.[1] For others, discovery of the kingdom will be part of a serious quest for things of ultimate value, something that, once discovered, fulfils their lifelong quest.

Whichever is the case, two things are important to note. The first is that the kingdom of God is something we *find*, it is not something we earn or deserve. It is pure grace, something God does and we discover, not something *we* create by our own effort. And secondly, and most importantly, it is not only *finding* the kingdom that counts but also *recognising* its full significance and inestimable value. If the labourer and the merchant had not perceived the great value of what they found, their discovery would have been to no effect.

All Christians would claim to have found in Jesus the reality of God's kingdom, and would understand this discovery as being 'altogether by grace.' But I wonder whether, having found the kingdom, we all truly recognise its *great worth and immense significance*. It is noteworthy that these two parables in Matthew's Gospel are addressed to the disciples, to

---

1   Derrett comments that, whilst not wanting to derive too much significance from the differences between the two stories, 'it is perhaps legitimate to claim that they show that Jesus wanted to give information about the kingdom through pictures of a variety of "findings" by "finders" of a variety of qualifications and situations,' *Law in the New Testament*, 14. Similarly A.M. Hunter comments 'surely this reveals Jesus' awareness that it is often by very different roads that men come to the kingdom,' *Interpreting the Parables* (London: SCM, 1964), 65. Jeremias, on the other hand, maintains that 'the difference between the method of discovery in each case . . . is irrelevant . . . In both parables the discovery is a surprise.' *Parables*, 200. Similarly, F.W. Beare, *The Gospel According to Matthew* (Oxford: Basil Elack, 1981), 314f

those who had already embraced Jesus (cf. v.36). Jesus was encouraging his committed followers[1] — believers, not unbelievers — to perceive the ultimate and far-reaching significance of what God was doing through him; to recognise, hidden behind the unimpressive trappings of his own life and ministry, God's ultimate self-revelation; to perceive in his ministry that God was secretly acting to bring the whole of creation back under God's perfect rule. If they could truly 'see' the kingdom of God for what it is, Jesus says, it would revolutionise their lives forever.

The same applies to us. We can have a terribly impoverished understanding of what God has accomplished in the life, death and resurrection of Christ. The message of the gospel is awe-inspiring in its proportions; it is staggering in its dimensions! It is not simply that God wants to save a few disembodied souls; it's not simply about making people happy or getting them into heaven when they die. It includes this of course, but it is much, much more.

The good news of the kingdom of God is that God has acted to save the world, to heal creation, to bring the whole of life back under God's perfect reign. In the incarnation, and in the life, death and resurrection of Christ, we have an unshakeable guarantee that *God does not intend to trash this planet; God intends to refurbish it.* God intends to purge the world of

---

1   Many scholars, following Kingsbury's analysis of the narrative strategy of chap 13, propose that Matt 13 is carefully structured so that 'the unresponsive crowds are . . . clearly distinguished from the disciples, ' R.T. France, *The Gospel According to Matthew* (Leicester: IVP, 1985), 216. Gundry argues that in the first parable, 'the field', which echoes vv.24 and 31, 'represents the world, throughout which God's rule extends in the discipling of all nations, ' and that *anthropos* is Matthew's term for a disciple, *Matthew*, 276

evil, to heal it of its wounds, and to restore it to the condition God intended for it at the beginning.

The gospel is cosmic in its scope; it embraces personal renewal, social renewal and ecological renewal. When God's kingdom comes in its fullness, there will be *shalom* or wholeness throughout all creation. Justice and peace shall embrace forever; the knowledge of God shall fill the earth as the waters cover the sea. And in Christ, the gospel declares, this process of personal and social and cosmic renewal has begun. It is *already* under way, and one day will most certainly be completed.

If God has acted in Christ to be reconciled to sinful humanity, then we must be passionately concerned to see men and women reconciled to God today. If God has acted in Christ to initiate a reign of peace, justice and righteousness, then we must *also* be passionately concerned for the creation of peace, justice and righteousness in the world now. We do a terrible disservice to the lordship of Christ if we confine our interest as Christians to narrowly defined 'spiritual' or 'religious' issues of life, and fail to ask what the gospel means for the political, economic, scientific, educational and artistic spheres of life as well. Christ is Lord of all — or he is not Lord at all. Our call as Christians, I believe, is to be representatives of and agents for God's redeeming work in the world — in *all* the world and in *all* the manifold activities of life.

That is the call of the gospel. The task of Christian leaders is to equip the people of God to be co-workers with God in the restoration of this rebellious and sinful world. If we are to be the salt and light that our lost, hurting and destructive society needs, we first need to discover the paramount significance of Jesus' proclamation of the kingdom of God to the whole of life and to all the problems and agonies of our world.

When we make that discovery, the Christian life becomes tremendously exciting. Instead of waiting passively around for God to beam us up to glory, to rescue us from this godforsaken world, we come to see our role as *active participants* in extending and expressing God's kingdom here in this (far from God-forsaken!) world. That's exciting stuff. Perhaps that's why, in the parable of the treasure, the result of finding the hidden treasure, of acquiring that priceless insight into the character and extent of God's redeeming work, is *joy*. 'Then in his joy he goes and sells all that he has and buys that field.'

Joy is a by-product of truth. When we grasp the truth of God, it always brings joy. The remarkable truth of what God has done and is doing in Christ should fill us with energising joy. One of our biggest problems as Christians, one the main reasons why the Christian community sometimes seems so ineffectual and innocuous, is that we do not always believe what we preach. If we really believed, with all our hearts and souls, the truth of the gospel — that in Jesus God has acted to redeem the world, and this work of redemption *will* one day most certainly be completed — it would radicalise the way we live.

Do we really believe that the way of Christ, which can seem so weak and foolish in the world's eyes, will ultimately triumph? Do we really believe that good is stronger than evil; that love is stronger than violence; that forgiveness is stronger than hatred? Does the robust truthfulness of the gospel message fill us with joy?

A Remarkable Response

The man who found the hidden treasure was filled with joy. And in his joy, he radically changed his whole manner of life. He made a remarkable response to his remarkable discovery. The proof that we have recognised the awe-inspiring reality and significance of Christ's kingdom is not only joy, but the way this joy works itself out concretely in practice, the way it affects our lifestyle.

In both stories, the finders of the hidden wealth respond in two ways: they *sell* all that they possess, and they *buy* the treasure they have found. The repetition of the verbs 'sell' and 'buy' in both stories underscores the significance of these actions.

Very frequently in Jesus' teaching, commitment to discipleship involves selling or leaving one's possessions in order to identify wholly with Jesus. Remember his words to the rich young ruler: 'There is one thing still lacking; *sell all that you own and distribute the money to the poor,* and you will have treasure in heaven; then come, follow me'.[1] Or his words to the disciples: 'Do not be afraid, little flock, for it is your Father's good pleasure to give you the kingdom. *Sell your possessions* and give alms. Make purses for yourselves that do not wear out, an unfailing treasure in heaven, where no thief comes near and no moth destroys. For where your *treasure* is, there will your heart be also.'[2] Or again, 'none of you can become my disciple if you do not *give up all your possessions.*'[3]

---

1   Luke 18:22
2   Luke 12:32-34
3   Luke 14:33

We frequently overlook or seriously dilute this oft-repeated feature of Jesus' teaching. This is not the place to explore it fully, but I want to suggest that Jesus' basic concern was that his disciples *disinvested* themselves from the existing order of things in the world, and *reinvested* themselves wholly in the service of God's kingdom.

The kingdom of God, in the Gospels, is all about God exerting kingly power, through Jesus, to put right what is wrong in the world; to initiate a process of redemption that will climax in the renewal and renovation of the world. What the Jews expected to happen in one fell swoop at the end of history, Jesus claimed was beginning to happen, in a secret hidden way, in advance of the End, in and through his own ministry. God was not waiting till the end of time to renew the world. God's saving, renewing power had already invaded the present age in Jesus, bringing forgiveness and healing and deliverance, creating a new community that lived a new way of life, a community that embodied the peace and justice of God's kingdom. The future had invaded the present.

Now it is important to understand God's strategy for redeeming the world. The strategy has not been to *replace* the existing world order with an entirely new order, but to begin a new creation in the midst of fallen creation; to plant the seeds of change in the midst of the old order; to establish a 'colony of the new age' (H.C. Kee) in the midst of the old age. For this strategy to be effective, the people of God must be wholeheartedly committed to God's new order. Christians must allow their lives, their values and priorities, their relationships and commitments, their possessions and vocations, to be fundamentally shaped by the demands of God's kingdom, not by the standards of this world. *We are meant to be different from the world around us.* We are meant to be a visible demonstration that God has made a whole new way of life possible. *We are meant to be the showcase of God's future.*

The tragedy is, of course, that we Christians often resemble the society we live in much more than we resemble God's new society. We preach the gospel and proclaim God's kingdom, but we invest ourselves, our time, our energies, our dollars, in maintaining the existing order. The danger is that if we become too comfortable with the world as it is, if we benefit too much from the status quo, if we allow the world around us 'to squeeze us into its mould',[1] we will cease to be agents for change. We will cease to pray for and work towards the *transformation* of society in the name of God's reign.

That, in my view, is what the idea of selling and buying means in these two little parables, and elsewhere in Jesus' teaching. We are to surrender our personal and material investment in the world as it is, and commit ourselves, and all our personal and material resources, to the work of God's kingdom in the world. We are to 'seek first God's kingdom, and God's righteousness,' and deploy all that we are and all that we possess in service of God's work of renewing and changing the world, in the name of Christ.

---

1   Rom 12:2 (Phillips)

About the Author

*P*rofessor Chris Marshall is currently holder of the Diana Unwin Chair in Restorative Justice in the School of Government, at Victoria University of Wellington, New Zealand. Prior to taking up this post in *2014*, he was the St John's Professor of Christian Theology and Head of the School of Art History, Classics and Religious Studies at Victoria University. Before that he taught New Testament for 19 years at Laidlaw College in Auckland, during which time he wrote *Kingdom Come* for use by his students.

In addition to *Kingdom Come* (1990), Marshall is author of *Faith As a Theme In Mark's Narrative* (Cambridge University Press, 1989), *Beyond Retribution: A New Testament Vision For Justice, Crime, and Punishment* (Wm. B. Eerdmans, 2001), *Crowned With Glory And Honor: Human Rights In The Biblical Tradition* (Pandora Press, 2001), *Little Book Of Biblical Justice* (Good Books, 2005) and *Compassionate Justice: An Interdisciplinary Dialogue with Two Gospel Parables on Law, Crime, and Restorative Justice* (Cascade: Wipf & Stock, 2012).

Printed in Great Britain
by Amazon